The LightFoot Companion to the via Francigena

ITALY

Great Saint Bernard Pass to St Peter's Square, Rome

ISBN 978-2-917183-38-0

www.pilgrimagepublications.com

ALSO BY LIGHTFOOT GUIDES

LightFoot Guide to the via Francigena
- Canterbury to the Great Saint Bernard Pass, Switzerland
- the Great Saint Bernard Pass Switzerland to St Peter's, Rome, Italy

LightFoot Guide to the via Domitia, Arles to Vercelli

LightFoot Companion
- to the via Francigena - Italy
- to the Via Francigena - England, France and Switzerland
- to the via Domitia

LightFoot Guide to the Three Saints' Way
- Winchester to Mont St Michel
- Mont St Michel to St Jean d'Angely

LightFoot Guide to Foraging
- A guide to over 130 of the most common edible and medicinal plants in Western Europe

LightFoot Guide to the via Podiensis
- An up-to-date and complete guide to the 774 kilometre journey from Le Puy-en-Velay to the Pyrenees

Your Camino
- Information, maps for Camino routes in France and Spain

Camino Lingo
- A cheats' guide to speaking Spanish on the Camino

Slackpacking the Camino Frances
- All the information and advice you'll need to plan your perfect Camino

Author's note - A book of this type can be never complete. Feedback and suggestions are always welcomed. mail@pilgrimagepublications.com

LA VIA FRANCIGENA

CANTERBURY-ROME

VIII	SCE REMEI	SAINT-RHEMY-EN-BOSSES
XLV	EVERI	IVREA
XLIV	SCA AGATHA	SANTHIA
XLIII	VERCEL	VERCELLI
XLII	TREMEL	TROMELLO
XLI	PAMPHICA	PAVIA
XL	SCE CRISTINE	SANTA CRISTINA E BISSONE
XXXIX	SCE ANDREA	CORTE SAN ANDREA
XXXVIII	PLACENTIA	PIACENZA
XXXVII	FLORICUM	FIORENZUOLA D'ARDA
XXXVI	SCE DOMNINE	FIDENZA
XXXV	METANE	COSTAMEZZANA
XXXIV	PHILEMANGENUR	FORNOVO DI TARO
XXXIII	SCE MODERANNE	BERCETO
XXXII	SCE BENEDICTE	MONTELUNGO
XXXI	PUNTREMEL	PONTREMOLI
XXX	AGUILLA	AULLA
XXIX	SCE STEPHANE	SANTO STEFANO DI MAGRA
XXVIII	LUNA	LUNI
XXVII	CAMPMAIOR	PIEVE DI CAMAIORE
XXVI	LUCA	LUCCA
XXV	FORCRI	PORCARI
XXIII	AQUA NIGRA	PONTE A CAPPIANO

XXIII	ARNE BLANCA	FUCECCIO
XXII	SCE DIONISII	SAN GENESIO
XXI	SCE PETER CURRANT	COIANO
XX	SCE MARIA GLAN	SANTA MARIA A CHIANNI
XIX	SCE GEMIANE	SAN GIMIGNANO
XVIII	SCE MARTIN IN FOSSE	SAN MARTINO FOSCI
XVII	AELSE	GRACCIANO
XVI	BURGENOVE	BADIA AN ISOLA
XV	SEOCINE	SIENA
XIV	ARBIA	PONTE D'ARBIA
XIII	TURREINER	TORRENIERI
XII	SCE QUIRIC	SAN QUIRICO D'ORCIA
XI	ABRICULA	BRICCOLE DI SOTTO
X	SCE PETIR IN PAIL	SAN PIETRO IN PAGLIA
IX	AQUAPENDENTE	ACQUAPENDENTE
VIII	SCA CRISTINA	BOLSENA
VII	SCE FLAVIANE	MONTEFIASCONE
VI	SCE VALENTINE	VITERBO
V	FURCARI	VETRALLA
IIII	SUTERIA	SUTRI
III	BACANE	BACCANO
II	JOHANNIS VIIII	SAN GIOVANNI IN NONO
I	URBS ROMA	ROMA

Contents

To be a Pilgrim

Who would true valour see,
Let him come hither;
One here will constant be,
Come wind, come weather.
There's no discouragement
Shall make him once relent
His first avowed intent,
To be a pilgrim.

Whoso beset him round
With dismal stories
Do but themselves confound;
His strength the more is.
No lion can him fright,
He'll with a giant fight,
But he will have a right
To be a pilgrim.

Hobgoblin, nor foul fiend,
Can daunt his spirit:
He knows, he at the end
Shall life inherit.
Then fancies fly away,
He'll fear not what men say,
He'll labour night and day
To be a pilgrim.

John Bunyan

Pilgrims and Pilgrimages

The epitome of the Medieval travelling man, the *homo viator,* was the pilgrim who embarked on a journey towards one of Christianity's holy destinations. The practice of peregrination was presented as an example of faith and charity, linked to the metaphor of our journey towards the ultimate spiritual and heavenly goal. The main destinations were Rome, Jerusalem and Santiago de Compostela, carried out on foot, with the help of nothing more than a *burdon* - a term originally referring to mules and later to the pilgrim staff. In addition, pilgrims carried a cloak, wide-brimmed hat and a haversack or purse slung around the waist. Various illustrations and paintings depict a type of dressing ceremony with the bestowal of a blessing by the bishop before departure, but this was probably reserved for people of high rank. The Medieval sense of hospitality derives from a Christian concept of offering material and spiritual aid to one's fellow-man. Hospitals were modeled on monastic settlements and existed as permanent religious institutions often run by monastic orders. The codes of behaviour and rules observed inside the institution also applied to the guests for the duration of their stay. Only the wealthier hospitals in towns and in the most important institutions provided beds and food, while others restricted their hospitality to the primary necessities, straw to lie on and religious succour.

In addition to the support provided by religious organisations, based on the concept of *Misericordia* (the Latin translation of the Hebrew word *hesed,* meaning loving-kindness), there were other hostels of a secular nature, such as inns and, in some cases, spas, but these were usually frequented by a wealthier clientèle - merchants and knights who carried money with them and attracted brigands to such an extent that the municipal authorities were finally forced to intervene to protect all travellers, including the less wealthy pilgrims.

Pilgrim - person who journeys to a sacred place; a traveller or wanderer.
Peregrini - those who go through fields (*per agros*), transients.

The Labyrinth

Christianity adopted the labyrinth as a symbol in the Middle Ages, changing the design to imbue it with specifically Christian meaning. The earliest known example is from a 4th century pavement in the Basilica of St Reparatus, Orleansville, Algeria, which is marked with the words *Sancta Eclesia* at its centre, though it is unclear how it might have been used in worship.

This movement sustained until the 18th century, when the essentially pagan origins of the labyrinth were recognised, with the result that many were destroyed. Opinions as to the function and meaning of the old church labyrinths vary. Some maintain they were merely introduced as a symbol of the perplexities and intricacies of the Christian's path. Alternatively, it is asserted that the larger examples were used for the performance of miniature pilgrimages as a substitution for the long and tedious journeys. Some credence is given to this supposition by the name *Chemin de Jérusalem,* which is given to the vast labyrinth in Chartres cathedral. The accompanying ritual, supposedly involving pilgrims following the maze on their knees while praying, may have been practiced there during the 17th century. The full flowering of the Medieval labyrinth came about from the 12th through to the 14th centuries with the grand pavement labyrinths of the Gothic cathedrals, notably Chartres, Reims and Amiens. The cathedral labyrinths are thought to be the inspiration for the many turf mazes, such as survive at Wing, Hilton, Alkborough, and Saffron Walden in the United Kingdom.

Labyrinths along the via Francigena

Reims Cathedral, France
San Michele Maggiore, Pavia, Italy
San Pietro de Conflentu, Pontremoli, Italy
Lucca Cathedral, Italy

The via Francigena Yesterday and Today

Omnes via e Romam Perducunt' All roads lead to Rome …

The via Francigena is not a single road, but a collection of several possible routes, which changed over the centuries as trade and the pilgrimage culture developed and waned. Depending on the time of year, political situation, and relative popularity of the shrines of saints along the route, travellers may have used any of three or four crossings over the Alps and the Apennines. First documented as the Lombard Way and later the *Iter Francorum*, the via Francigena was only mentioned as such in the *Actum Clusi*, a parchment produced in 876 in the Abbey of San Salvatore al Monte Amiata (Tuscany). Then, at the end of the 10th century, Sigeric the Serious, Archbishop of Canterbury, used the via Francigena to travel to Rome for his consecration by the Pope. He recorded his return journey, and the places where he stopped, in a document which is now held in the British Library, but nothing in it suggests that the route was new. His itinerary lists the seventy-nine *submansiones*, which define the via Francigena as we know it today. Many reports of journeys before and after Sigeric can only be apocryphal, but we can be certain that St Thierry, known as William of St Thierry, used the roads towards Rome on several occasions at the end of the 11th century. Other itineraries include those of the Icelandic traveller Nikolás Bergsson in 1154, and Philip Augustus of France, who entered Italy, via Moncenisio, in 1191. Subsequent accounts also cite the pass over Montgenévre and through the Susa Valley as a route used by both Pilgrims travelling to Rome (along what is now recognised as a branch of the via Francigena), and armies invading Italy. In the 12th century, the increase in commercial relations between Italy and the Germanic areas led to a renewed use of the passes in the central and eastern Alps, like the St Gotthard and Brenner passes. In the 13th century trade grew to such an extent that several alternative routes

to the via Francigena were developed, and it consequently lost its unique character and broke into numerous different routes linking the north and Rome. Also, the walking paths and trails often linked monasteries instead, of major cities, and by the 16th Century there were more direct routes. Nevertheless, the via Francigena route described by Sigeric was still in frequent use, as evidenced in the journey of Barthelemy Bonis, a merchant of Montauban who took part in the Jubilee of 1350, having survived the plague of 1348. Other documents also record Charles VIII's journey along the via Francigena in1494, as part of his armed descent on Naples.

Today, the number of modern pilgrims on the via Francigena is very small compared to Medieval times, the heyday of long-distance pilgrimage in Europe. However, the via Francigena has been slowly rediscovered in recent years, particularly since the route was given the title of European Cultural Route by the Council of Europe, in 1994, meaning more resources and funds were allocated to maintain, mark and promote the trail; particularly by the Italian Government. In 2007 a 0km milestone was laid outside Canterbury Cathedral, the official starting point.

People who follow the via Francigena can make of it what they will. A religious, spiritual, cerebral experience, a precious opportunity to discover Europe and the cultures along the route, a physical challenge, or all of the above, but they will be doing so with minimal environmental impact, and hopefully maximum understanding of the people they meet along the way.

"*There never was a pilgrim who did not come back to his village with one less prejudice and one more idea.*"

François-René de Chateaubriand

François-René de Chateaubriand

The French writer and historian set out from Paris in July 1806, his ultimate goal, Jerusalem. On his return to France, he wrote the *Itinéraire de Paris à Jérusalem*, which was published in 1811, and described as the most widely read book on Palestine in the early 19th century. The high point of Chateaubriand's pilgrimage was when he was made a knight of the Holy Sepulchre at the site of Christ's tomb, with the sword of Godfrey of Bouillon. He described his motivation when he said: "I will perhaps be the last Frenchman leaving my country to voyage to the Holy Land with the ideas, feelings and aims of a pilgrim."

A conduit for cultural and artistic change

The extent to which the via Francigena facilitated all forms of exchange between communities is well known, one of the clearest examples being in art and culture. How else can we explain the vestment made from traditional Persian *samite* (a luxurious and heavy silk fabric often including gold or silver thread) dating back to the Carolingian age? Or the *Codex Amiatinus*, an 8th century English Bible and the Vercelli Book, left there by a Scotic pilgrim in the 6th century?

Similarly, architects and builders were clearly open to the external influences brought in by the via Francigena. Tightly woven exchanges can be seen between the Lombard Romanesque style, or more generically that of the Po region and France. A prime example of this can be found in the work of Nicolao, a sculptor who, between 1120 and 1140, was working on the abbey of San Michele della Chiusa in Piacenza, obviously inspired by the Wiligelmic tradition, but also by the art of the Aquitaine. In Tuscany, where French architectural styles are evident in buildings both along and near the via Francigena, the abbey church of Sant'Antimo is the only one to have a basilica plan, complete with the aisle and side chapels typical of the great pilgrimage churches in France and Santiago de Compostela.

Sigeric the Serious - Archbishop of Canterbury

Nothing in his history identifies Sigeric (990–994) as being more serious than anyone else at the time. The epithet may have originated from his learning, or could have been derived from transliteration of his name into Latin as *Serio.*

Sigeric took holy orders at Glastonbury Abbey, where he was educated and subsequently elected Abbot of St Augustine's. In approximately 986 he was consecrated to the See of Ramsbury and Sonning, and finally transferred to the See of Canterbury in 990. Today, Sigeric's only real claim to fame is his journey from Rome to Canterbury. After receiving his cope and *pallium* (a circular band of white wool with pendants, worn by archbishops) from the Pope, Sigeric recorded his return journey, listing the places he passed through and identifying them as *submansiones*, but he was also notable for a number of decisive acts for which future generations should be grateful.

While Sigeric was an abbot, Ælfric dedicated a book of translated homilies to him and advised King Æthelred to found Cholsey Abbey in Berkshire, in honour of King Edward the Martyr, as well as having Edward memorialized at Shaftesbury Abbey. Later, in 991, it was Sigeric who advised King Æthelred to pay a tribute to the invading Danish king, Sweyn Forkbeard. Æthelred presented Sweyn with 10,000 pounds of silver and in response Sweyn temporarily ceased his destructive advance into England, though he did return later for a further tribute. Sweyn's ever-increasing demands in the following years resulted in a debilitating tax known as the *Danegeld*, payable by the inhabitants of Æthelred's territories. In 994, Sigeric paid tribute to the Danes and secured the protection of Canterbury Cathedral.

Sigeric died on 28 October 994 and was buried in Christ Church, Canterbury. His Last Will and Testament left wall hangings to Glastonbury as well as a valuable collection of books to his church in Sonning.

The via Francigena in Italy

I reached the Alps: the soul within me burned,
Italia, my Italia, at thy name:
And when from out the mountain's heart I came
And saw the land for which my life had yearned,
I laughed as one who some great prize had earned:
And musing on the marvel of thy fame
I watched the day, till marked with wounds of flame
The turquoise sky to burnished gold was turned.
The pine-trees waved as waves a woman's hair,
And in the orchards every twining spray
Was breaking into flakes of blossoming foam:
But when I knew that far away at Rome
In evil bonds a second Peter lay,
I wept to see the land so very fair.

Oscar Wilde

Italy comprises a remarkable kaleidoscope of regions, landscapes and cultures. Extending over 1,000 kilometres it stretches from the far northern reaches, which take in the Alps, the industrialised Po plain, all the way down to sun-soaked Mediterranean shores and islands of the south. The term *Italia* is thought to have originated from the ancient tribe name *Itali*, though another, more common explanation is that the term was borrowed from the Greek word *Víteliú*, meaning land of young cattle. The bull was a symbol of the southern Italian tribes and often depicted goring the Roman wolf as a defiant symbol of free Italy during the Samnite Wars. Italy shares its northern, Alpine boundary with France, Switzerland, Austria and Slovenia. The independent states of San Marino and the Vatican City are enclaves within the Italian Peninsula, and Campione d'Italia is an Italian ex-clave in Switzerland. Italy's capital, Rome, was for centuries, the political centre of Western civilisation and the capital of the Roman Empire. After its decline, Italy endured numerous invasions from Germanic tribes such as the Lombards and Ostrogoths, to the Normans and later, the Byzantines, among others.

Italy is probably most strongly associated with art, culture and more specifically, the Renaissance. One could argue that the fuel for this rebirth was the rediscovery of ancient texts that had been almost forgotten by Western civilization, but were preserved in monastic or private libraries. Renaissance scholars scoured the libraries in search of works by classical authors such as Plato, Cicero and Vitruvius - works that were diffused into the Christian world, providing new intellectual material for European scholars.

The Black Death pandemic in 1348 left its mark on Italy, killing one third of the population, but ultimately the recovery actually led to a resurgence of cities, trade and economy, which greatly stimulated the successive phase of the Humanism and Renaissance (15th-16th centuries), when Italy again resumed its status as the centre of Western civilization, strongly influencing the other European countries with Courts like Este in Ferrara and De Medici in Florence. Through much of its post-Roman history, Italy was fragmented into numerous kingdoms and city-states, but unified in 1861, following a tumultuous period in history known as the *Risorgimento*. In the late 19th century, Italy gained a colonial empire, which extended its rule to Libya, Eritrea, Italian Somalia and Ethiopia, Albania, Rhodes, the Dodecanese and a concession in Tianjin, China.

Today, modern Italy is a democratic republic, founding member of what is now the European Union, and home to more than sixty-two million individuals, as of 2017. Italian culture is steeped in the arts, family, architecture, music and food. The major religion in Italy is Roman Catholicism, which is not surprising, because Vatican City is the hub of Roman Catholicism and where the Pope resides. Roman Catholics and other Christians make up eighty percent of the population, while Muslim, agnostic and atheist make up the other twenty percent. Italy has given rise to a number of architectural styles, including classical Roman, Renaissance, Baroque and Neoclassical, and is home to some of the most famous structures in the world, including the Colosseum in Rome and the Leaning Tower of Pisa. The concept of a basilica - which was originally used to describe an open public court building and evolved to mean a Catholic pilgrimage site - was born in Italy.

The Aosta Valley

The Italian section of the via Francigena starts in the Aosta Valley, one of Italy's smallest regions, in terms of area, and one of the least populated, due, in part, to its rugged terrain. Italy's northern regions were at times French, Austrian, and Italian, and although the Aosta Valley hasn't been in French hands since the mid-1500s, proximity alone means that it still has a split personality. There are two official names for the region – one Italian, one French. The local language is more French than anything else and many towns in the region have French names. It was only under Duke Emmanuele Filiberto in the 16th century that the region was brought definitively into the Italian sphere of influence, and later played a key role in the *Risorgimento,* the ambitious movement that united Italy. The vestiges of this history are to be found in the Medieval castles and *sacri monti* around the foothills of the Alps.

The mountains alone did not provide sufficient protection to the fragmented kingdoms in the Aosta valley, meaning the Medieval lords who ruled ruthlessly over their small domains had to build castles to enforce their often fragile power. Originally, Aosta's castles were designed to be defensive and threatening, but the castles of Fénis and Verrés, represent an important shift in the function of the feudal castle. As you continue along the valley look out for the Medieval Tower of Gignod.

Having crossed the border into Italy, and made the steep descent from the summit, you will trace the route taken by popes and pilgrims, common wayfarers and noble leaders, and even Napoleon's army. Your first pause may well be in Saint-Rhemy-en-Bosses, which Sigeric also listed as one of his stopping places.

Saint-Rhémy-en-Bosses XLVIII Sce Remei

Set deep in the sunny valley, which stretches to the foot of the Great Saint Bernard mountain, Saint-Rhémy-en-Bosses is a small village centred around an ancient bridge connecting Italy and Northern Europe. Though its name originates from the day when King Guntram was christened by Saint Remi of Reims, in 496AD, the village itself dates back to Roman times when it was a toll post on the road into the Aosta valley.

Of particular interest:

Bosses Castle, built in 1095 by Gerardo de Bocha, a local Lord who owned all the feudal justice rights. The present three-storey building with rectangular floor, probably dates back to the 15th century. The inside was restored and can be visited when exhibitions and events take place in it.

Fonte di Citrin, a fountain located in the square in front of the town hall, is famous for its healing, iron based water that flows down 1800 metres from the valley of the same name. If you pass through in July, you may be able to enjoy the traditional *Jambon de Bosses* food festival, a celebration of the famous, uncooked ham seasoned in the mountain pastures of the area. On the last Sunday of the festival, the locals dress in traditional costumes and parade through the town's streets.

Etroubles

Etroubles is a small town identified by its cobbled roads, springs, stone-tiled roofs and flower-filled balconies. In Roman times, it was known as *Restapolis* and was the main centre in the Great Saint Bernard valley. It probably housed the local garrison that guarded the main access from Gaul. To keep the traditional spirit alive, the life of the valley is animated by a number of folkloric events, such as the Carnival of Coumba Freide and Summer Veillà, an exhibition of historic handicraft, enlivened by dancers and singers from the region.

Aosta XLVII Agusta

For the Romans, Aosta's position at the confluence of two rivers and at the end of the Great and the Little St Bernard Pass, gave it considerable military importance. Its layout was that of a Roman military camp and today the ancient town walls of *Augusta Praetoria Salassorum* are still preserved. Towers stand at angles to the *enceinte* (a French term used to describe the inner ring of fortifications surrounding a town), and others are positioned at intervals, with two at each of the four gates, making twenty towers in total. The east and south gates are also still intact. The former, a double gate with three arches flanked by two towers is known as the *Porta Praetoria* (1st century AD). Apart from the marble covering, the gate is preserved in its original form.

Rich in monuments from pre-historical, Roman, Medieval and later times there is a lot to see and **of particular interest:**

The forum Cryptoporticus. Nobody has determined for sure what it was built for. Some say it was a walkway or a covered market, others believe it was a military granary. The mystery adds to its charm.

Aosta Cathedral features amazing Ottanian frescoes and a wooden choir. Its origins are associated with the initial stages of the diffusion of Christianity in the region. The great rebuilding of the 11th century involved important craftsmen and painters, who decorated the walls of the nave. The new marble high altar, by Lugano sculptor Francesco Albertolli, was installed in the mid-18th century, while the Neoclassical façade designed by the architect Gayo (1846–48) and the Neogothic chapel dedicated to the Holy Rosary (1862) are dated a century later.

Sant'Orso, or Saint-Ours, dedicated to Saint Ursus of Aosta, was entirely rebuilt during the 9th century. Fragments of a Romanesque series of paintings are preserved in good condition in the space between the current vault and the original ceiling. These portray scenes from the New Testament as well as a martyrdom. The cloister is enchanting and perfect for quiet reflection. The church is home to numerous missals and reliquaries, including the relics of Ursus, which rest in the crypt. It also holds the relics of Saint Gratus of Aosta.

Fenis Castle

Though not directly on the route, you will see Fenis castle dominating the other side of the valley. It first appears in a document in 1242 AD as a property of the Viscounts of Aosta, the Challant family. At that time it was probably a simple keep surrounded by walls, but from 1320 AD to 1420 AD, under the lordship of Aimone of Challant and of his son Bonifacio of Challant, the castle expanded. They gave it the distinctive pentagonal layout, external boundary wall and many of the towers. Then, in 1392, Bonifacio of Challant began a second building campaign to build the staircase and the balconies in the inner courtyard and the prison. He also commissioned Piedmontese painter, Giacomo Jaqueiro, to paint frescoes on the chapel and in the inner courtyard. Under Bonifacio I, the castle reached its greatest splendour, with a luxurious centre court surrounded by a vegetable plot, a vineyard and a garden where the lord and his guests could relax.

Fenis castle belonged to the lords of Challant until 1716, when Georges François of Challant had to sell it to Count Baldassarre, Castellar of Saluzzo Paesana, in order to pay his debts. From here, it went through a period of neglect, during which it was turned into a rural dwelling and became a stable and barn. Fortunately, architect Alfredo d'Andrade purchased it in 1895 and started a restoration campaign. In 1935 a second campaign by De Vecchi and Mesturino completed the restoration, and gave the castle its current appearance. Today, Fenis castle is owned by the Regional Council, which has turned it into a museum.

Verres Castle

The route takes you through Verrès and past Verrès Castle, a military fortress, built by Yblet de Challant in the 14th century. The castle stands on a rocky promontory, dominating the town access to the Val d'Ayas. From the outside it looks like an austere cube, thirty metres long on each side and practically free of decorative elements, but it is one of the most visited monuments of the Aosta Valley.

Every element of the castle seems to have been considered to make the fortress more defensible. If you visit it, you will climb a steep mule track, which winds up the mountain until it reaches the entrance in the circuit wall, accessed by means of a drawbridge.

On the death of Yblet, in 1409, the castle and his other possessions passed to his son François de Challant. François died in 1442, without male heirs, and left his property to his daughters Marguerite and Catherine. Verrès castle became one of the strongholds of Catherine and her husband Pierre Sarriod d'Introd. Legend has it that, on Trinity Sunday, 1449, Catherine and Pierre left the castle and went down to the town square, where they danced with the local people. Every year, the event is celebrated in May with a four-day carnival, which involves a procession, masquerade balls, and the performance of Giuseppe Giacosa's play, *Una Partita a Scacchi* (A Game of Chess).

Pont St Martin XLVI Publei

Although a pretty enough town, the main reason for lingering here is the bridge, an impressive testimony to Romanisation in Valle d'Aosta. Its date is uncertain. Some say it was built around 120 B.C., while others say 25 B.C. The wooden beam bearings dug into the rock can be seen at its base, though iron crowns were added at the end of the 19th century to strengthen the structure. A later dated legend ascribes the construction of the bridge to the devil. The story goes that St. Martin, the Bishop of Tours, was returning to his diocese when the Lys River overflowed and blocked the only footpath. The devil offered to resolve the problem by building a bridge in one night, but in return requested the soul of the first living being to cross it. The saint accepted, but the following morning he threw a piece of bread to the other side of the bridge, thus ensuring that a starving dog was the first to cross. The infuriated devil disappeared into the Lys with bolts of lightning and a sulphury stench, leaving the bridge to the local population.

Bard castle

Far from being a castle, it is in fact a forbidding 19th century fortress cascading down the hillside into a gorge. Originally, there was another fortress on this spot, guarding the entrance to the entire Aosta valley region. In 1800, 40,000 of Napoleon's troops swooped down across the Alps and besieged it. The garrison held out for fifteen days, and when they finally surrendered they were awarded honours by their victors.

The local nobility, the House of Savoy, later built the present fortress between 1830 and 1838, since when it has never actually been attacked. The current appearance of the fort is the result of reconstruction work that turned it into one of the largest military structures in the Aosta Valley. In the 19th century, it was used as a prison, then as a weapons depot and finally purchased by the Aosta Valley regional authority in 1990. In 2006, the castle was completely restored and now hosts the Museum of the Alps, and the Fortresses and Frontiers Museum, as well as other permanent and temporary exhibitions.

Et l'on peut dire sans exagération que c'est un des plus solides et plus fameux batiments qu'un vassal ait pu faire construire dans le domaine d'un prince souverain où celluy-cy tient le rang d'un des plus renommés.

And one can say without exaggeration that it is one of the most solid and most famous bastions that a vassal could have built in the domain of a sovereign prince – within which it is one of the most renowned.

Jean-Baptiste de Tillier

Piedmont

The Italian section of the via Francigena starts in Piedmont, Italy's second largest region. The name derives from *Pedemontium* or *Pedemontis*,

meaning at the foot of the mountains, and Piedmont is indeed surrounded on three sides by the Alps, which include the 3,841 meter high Monviso and Monte Rosa, the second highest mountain in the Alps.

At the border with France and Switzerland, the land slopes down from the highest peaks to the gentle hills of the Langhe and Monferrato, Piedmont's wine country, and to the Padan Plain, where the rice fields start. At the border with Lombardy, in the region's north-eastern portion is Lake Maggiore, Italy's second largest lake. The pleasant lakeside town of Stresa is the gateway to the Borromean islands. Piedmont's main city is Turin, which was the country's first capital.

Piedmont is one of Italy's leading gastronomic regions. The typical recipes of the area can be divided into two categories: those belonging to the noble tradition of the court of Savoy, and those born from more popular traditions. In the first case, we are talking about the very rich dishes served in the sumptuous court banquets such as boiled and fried mixed Piedmont meat, followed by chocolate and eggnog. In contrast, the recipes of the rural tradition are made with simple ingredients like *panissa*, and *Bagna cauda*, a warm dip served and eaten as a fondue.

A special mention must go to the cheeses, of which there are more than sixty types and of course the wines to accompany them. The Ancient Greeks started the grape growing tradition in Piedmont and, by the early 1500s, the wines of Piedmont were enjoyed in the papal court. Today, Piedmont is one of the most important Italian regions for both the quantity and the quality of wine produced.

Finally, Piedmont is also home to the *Sacri Monti* (Sacred Mountains), a group of devotional complexes, built on the slopes of a mountain during the late 16th and 17th centuries, which feature a series of chapels containing scenes from the life of Christ, the Virgin Mary and the Saints, in the form of paintings or sculptures. In 2003, they were named a World Heritage Site.

Ivrea XLV Everi

Ivrea and its surroundings have been inhabited since the Neolithic era. The Celts are believed to have had a village on the site from around the 5th century BC. However, the town first appears in history as a Roman cavalry station founded in 100 BC, and set to guard one of the traditional invasion routes into northern Italy over the Alps. The Latin name of the town, *Eporedia* (meaning a place to change horses), has long since vanished into the mists of time, but still appears as the root of the name of the town and the residents, who are known as *Porediesi,* in Italian, and as *Eporedians,* in English.

Later, Ivrea was a point of dispute between the bishops, the marquis of Monferrato and the House of Savoy. In 1356 the town was acquired by Amadeus VI of Savoy. With the exception of the brief French conquest at the end of the 16th century, Ivrea remained under Savoy until 1800.

There are two main festivals in Ivrea, both rooted in the ancient city's traditions. One is the Carnival, which takes place forty days before Easter, and ends on the night of Fat Tuesday with a solemn ceremony that involves

funeral in honour of the concluded Carnival. Though religious, the carnival is focused around the Battle of the Oranges, which involves thousands of townspeople, divided into nine teams, throwing oranges at each other, with considerable violence. The tradition is not well understood, particularly as oranges do not grow in the foothills of the Italian Alps and must be brought in, by the ton, from Sicily.

STORICO CARNEVALE DI IVREA®

The other festival is in honour of St. Savino, celebrated the week of July 7. This involves a horse fair, carriage exhibition and horse shows. But if you are not in Ivrea during the festivals there is a still a lot to see of historical and cultural interest in Ivrea.

Of particular interest:

Ivrea castle was built in 1358 at the behest of Amadeo VI of Savoy, the Conte Verde, as a symbol of the Savoy dominion over Ivrea and Canavese. Four massive circular towers characterise the structure, located next to the cathedral and the bishop's palace.

Ivrea's Cathedral is most noteworthy for its two towers, which are divided into several tiers with decorations and hanging arches. Beneath the main structure, the crypt contains an ancient Roman marble sarcophagus belonging to Quaestor Gaius Valerius Atecius, and three tombs of the ancient Bishops of the city.

The Bishop's Palace is thought to have been the home of Bishop Warmondo in the 10th century, but is actually a collection of buildings from different periods, though you should be able to see the remaining Medieval architectural features, such as the Bishop's Tower, which preserves some special terracotta decorations.

The Civic Museum is well worth visiting if you have time. Dedicated to the scholar Peter Alexander Garda (1791-1880), it has a section of Eastern and Archaeological art, and a number of frescoes from the 15th and 17th century.

One unexpected highlight is the Garda Collection of Oriental art. According to experts it is one of the most important collections outside Japan, and contains a great wealth of archaeological finds, mainly dedicated to the colony of Eporedia and its origins. Also in the museum, the Guelpa Collection includes a wide selection of paintings from the 14th to 20th centuries, such as the Crucifixion by Giovanni del Biondo (14th century), Madonna with the Child, by Neri di Bicci (1418-1492), Christ removed from the cross, attributed to Ambrogio da Fossano (1453-1523) and others. Art of the 20th century is represented by "Portrait of a woman" by Filadelfo Simi (1849-1923) and many works by Pietro Annigoni (1910-1988).

The Roman Amphitheatre, dating from the Late-Imperial Roman Age.

The Church of San Bernardino, with its frescoes depicting events from the "Life of Jesus". The oldest part of the church was built in the first half of the 15th century by the convent of the Franciscan order.

Santhia XLIVSca Agath

Santhià has been inhabited since the Roman period and is thought to have taken its name from Saint Agatha, a Christian martyr. Santhià is an agricultural centre where two branches of the via Francigena join: one towards the Great Saint Bernard Pass and the other towards the Vercelli.

Of particular interest:

The Church of Saint Agata dating back to the 10th Century.

Lake Viverone

Your route traces the shores of Lake Viverone named after the town. Wildlife, particularly mallard, coots, grebes and gulls thrive here. The lake is also an important archaeological site, with finds dating back to the Bronze Age. Leaving Viverone and the landscape dominated by the Alps, the route now crosses the Padana Plain and takes you through small forests that are home to pheasant and roe deer.

St Agatha

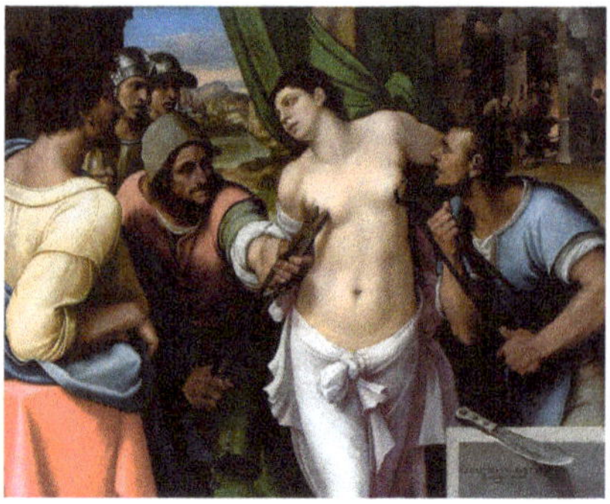

Born in Sicily and martyred in approximately 251 AD, St Agatha is one of seven women, excluding the Virgin Mary, commemorated by name in the Canon of the Mass. Rich and noble, she rejected the amorous advances of Quintianus, a Roman prefect, and as a result, was persecuted by him for her Christian faith. She was given to Aphrodisia, the keeper of a brothel and her nine daughters, but in response to their threats and entreaties to sacrifice to the idols and submit to Quintianus, Agata responded by saying: *"My courage and my thought be so firmly founded upon the firm stone of Jesus Christ, that for no pain it may not be changed; your words be but wind, your promises be but rain and your menaces be as rivers that pass and how well that all these things hurtle at the foundement of my courage, yet for that it shall not move."* After a number of other dramatic confrontations with Quintianus, her scorned admirer eventually sentenced her to death by being rolled naked on a bed of live coals.

Vercelli XLIII Vercel

Vercelli is one of the oldest urban sites in northern Italy, founded, according to most historians, around the year 600 BC. When Sigeric stopped off here, the area was covered by vast forests with some clearings, fields and marshes, but today it is the rice capital of Europe.

The world's first university funded by public money was established in Vercelli in 1228, but was closed in 1372. Today it has a university of literature and philosophy, as part of the Università del Piedmont Orientale, and a satellite campus of the Politecnico di Torino.

There is so much to see, and just wandering the streets is an experience in itself, but if you want to stop off and investigate its treasures in more detail, there are some options **of particular interest:**

Numerous relics of the Roman period: Amphitheatre, hippodrome, sarcophagi and many important inscriptions, some of which are Christian. Also two noteworthy towers: The Torre dell'Angelo and the Torre di Città in Via Gioberti.

The Museo Civico Borgogna is the best place to see the masterworks of the Vercelli school.

The Cathedral of Vercelli, was built centuries ago and remodelled several times. Ornately designed, the structure houses several very beautiful paintings by local artists. There is also a library in the cathedral, which holds a number of important ancient manuscripts, including the Laws of the Lombards from the 8th century, and the famous Vercelli Book, containing twenty-three homiletic or hagiographic texts in prose. Among these are six poems, the most well-known of which is The Dream of the Rood. Two of the other poems are signed by Cynewulf, a noted 8th century poet from northern Britain. The book is written in one hand and seems to be organised around themes, instead of according to the Church's liturgical calendar, as most homiliaries were. Although there is still much debate as to how the manuscript wound up in Italy, at least some sources give credence to the theory that Guala Bicchieri brought it back with him when he returned from England.

The basilica of Sant'Andrea was built in 1219 by Cardinal Guala

Bicchierie, along with an old monastery. Built in the Romanesque style of architecture, the monument is known to be one of the most well preserved and beautiful basilicas in Italy.

The Vercelli Synagogue, which dates back to 1878 and was designed by Marco Treves. A Moorish Revival synagogue with a striking white and red masonry designed to resemble synagogues in Europe and America.

If you are an art lover the Institute of the Beaux-Arts - which features a collection of paintings and art pieces by local artists collected over the centuries - is a must.

Cynewulf

One of twelve Old English poets known by that name, Cynewulf's work flourished during the 9th century and was best known for his religious compositions. Cynewulf was without question a literate and educated man and, given the subject matter of his poetry, it is also likely that he belonged to a holy order. His apparent reliance on Latin sources for inspiration also mean he knew the Latin language, which would correlate with him being a man of the Church.

All four of Cynewulf's poems contain passages where the letters of the poet's name are woven into the text using runic symbols, which also double as meaningful ideas pertinent to the text. The practice of claiming authorship over one's poems was a break from the tradition of the anonymous poet, where no composition was viewed as being owned by its creator, but Cynewulf's justification for doing so stemmed from the idea that poetry was associated with wisdom.

Then he who created this world...honoured us and gave us gifts... and also sowed and set in the mind of men many kinds of wisdom of heart. One he allows to remember wise poems, sends him a noble understanding, through the spirit of his mouth. The man whose mind has been given the art of wisdom can say and sing all kinds of things.

Guala Bicchieri

From a prominent family in Vercelli, Bicchieri trained for law but ultimately entered the clergy. He is first mentioned in 1187 as a canon in the cathedral of Vercelli, and by 1205 he had become a cardinal and served as a papal legate in northern Italy, before being appointed legate to France in 1208. Innocent III named him legate to England in, his mission being to make peace between the English and the French, because the civil war and the threat, by the French, to depose John from the English throne, were threatening Innocent's plan for a crusade. Guala's position as legate in England was especially influential because the Archbishop of Canterbury, Stephen Langton, was absent from September 1215 to May 1218, during which time Guala Bicchieri was to all intents and purposes in charge of the English church. Guala returned to Italy in 1219, after the final defeat of the English rebel barons and the Treaty of Lambeth. He founded the Abbey of St Andrew in Vercelli, his home town, named after the Abbey of Saint Andrew in Chesterton, which Bicchieri had been given for his services to the church during the difficult period of the civil war. In 1224, he also founded Saint Andrew's hospital in Vercelli.

Palestro

The route takes you through Palestro, an unremarkable town in itself, but very near the site of the Battle of Palestro, fought between the Austrian Empire and the combined forces of the Kingdom of Sardinia-Piedmont and France, in May 1859. The Franco-Piedmontese forces were victorious, and the day is also noteworthy for being the last time a monarch, Victor Emmanuel II in this case, rode into battle.

Lombardy

Next, the route takes you through Lombardy, a land of contrasts, stretching from the Alps, on the border with Switzerland, and down through the lakes of Como and Maggiore to the broad, flat plain of the Po River. The region is named Lombardia for the Lombards, the barbarian tribes that invaded the area in the 6th century AD. Archeological finds date the region's history back to the Etruscans and the Celts, then it underwent marked changes with the expansion of the Roman Empire in the 3rd century BC.

An area of lakeside villas and wealthy towns with imposing *palazzi*, highly decorated churches and modern industry alongside large-scale agriculture, Lombardy's centre is Milan, its style-conscious capital. The region has a long musical tradition. The composers, Giovanni Monteverdi and Donizetti and, violin maestro Antonio Stradivari, were all born in Piedmont, as was the classical poet, Virgil.

The regional cuisine of Lombardy is heavily based on ingredients like maize, rice, beef, pork, butter and lard, and has little in common with Central or Southern Italian dishes. A characteristic Lombard dish is risotto, most famously the *risotto alla milanese.* Similarly, maize-based dishes such as *polenta* are common parts of the regional cuisine. Other traditional dishes include *cotoletta, cassoeula* (braised pork and cabbage) and *ossobuco* (a different form of risotto). In addition, the region offers several delicacies and desserts, amongst which are *mostarda* (candied fruit with a mustard-flavoured syrup) and *panettone* (an Italian sweet bread). Regional cheeses include Robiola, Crescenza, Taleggio, Gorgonzola and Grana Padano.

The wine-making tradition of Lombardy dates back to its settlement by Greeks from Athens along the Po river. Archaeological evidence suggests that these settlers traded wine with the Etruscans in nearby Tuscany. The region is particularly known for its sparkling wines made in the Franciacorta, and produces red, white and rosé wines from a variety of local and international grapes.

Publius Vergilius Maro

Virgil was born on October 15, 70 BCE in Andes, a small village near Mantua, north of the Po River in Cisalpine Gaul. The son of a farmer, he was a classical Roman poet, best known for three major works - the Bucolics (or Eclogues), the Georgics, and the Aeneid, although several minor poems are also attributed to him.

Over the past three hundred years, much of Virgil's long-standard ancient biography, based on hearsay and legends, has been challenged. After Virgil's death, Romans and Italians attributed many myths to his tomb, contending that the cave in which he was buried was carved out by the supernatural power of his gaze.

His earliest poetry reveals a formidable literary training. The rustic tragedies of his Bucolics 1 and 9 are the stuff of life in Italy during the First Triumvirate (Julius Caesar, Pompey, and Crassus) and the Second Triumvirate (Mark Antony, Lepidus, and Octavian) and not necessarily autobiographical. Nevertheless, they show Virgil's concerns in his early career. The Bucolics were a hugely popular success and were performed on-stage for more than four hundred years after publication. They were also recited in the streets of Rome by Christian priests, who should have been reciting psalms.

Virgil became a major national figure, as well as a rich man. His estate being worth twenty-five times the property qualification of a Roman knight.

The date Virgil actually began the Aeneid is uncertain, but the proemium to the third Georgic (verses 21-39) suggests that he was thinking of writing an epic long before he actually began it, though he may not even have finished the Georgics before beginning the Aeneid. Heatstroke led to Virgil's death in 19 B.C., before the Aeneid was altogether finished.

Robbio

The area of Robbio has been settled since Neolithic times. As a Roman centre it was named *Redobium* and mentioned by Pliny the Elder. Later, the settlement was ceded to the Lombards and became a possession of the Catholic diocese of Vercelli. Around the 11th century, it was acquired by the De Robbio family, who ruled it and the neighbouring area until the 13th century, when it was contended between Vercelli and Pavia. In 1220 the latter definitively acquired Robbio through a diploma issued by Emperor Frederick II. Then part of the Duchy of Milan, it was entrusted to several feudal families. In 1748 it was acquired by the Kingdom of Sardinia and, in the 19th century, Robbio finally became part of the province of Pavia, under the newly formed Kingdom of Italy.

Of particular interest:

The Romanesque church of St. Peter, housing 16th century frescoes attributed to Tommasino da Mortara.

The 15th century church of San Michele, with a late Gothic-style façade.

Mortara

Quivi cader de' Longobardi tanti, e tanta fu quivi la strage loro, che 'l loco de la pugna gli abitanti Mortara dapoi sempre nominoro.	*Here several Longobards died and the slaughter of them was so great that, from then on, the inhabitants gave the place of the battle the name of Mortara.*
Ludovico Ariosto, I cinque canti - canto II, 88	

Originally named *Pulchra Silva* by the Romans, the settlement became Mortara after the bloody battle during which Charlemagne defeated the Longobard King Desiderius in 773. Set in the centre of flat, featureless rice fields, the town actually has a great deal to offer.

Of particular interest:

San Lorenzo, a Gothic basilica with a brick facade built by Bartolino da Novara, between 1375 and 1380, and restored in 1840 and in 1916. The portrait of SS. Albin, Amìcus and Amelius are 19th century copies from a 15th century polyptych by Paolo da Brescia, a work first presented in the church of San Albin, and now conserved in the Savoy picture-gallery in Turin. The church has several artistic masterpieces inside. From the right of the entrance, in the first span there is a 15th century fresco representing the Virgin with her Child. In the second span there is between Saints Roch and St. Sebastian, which some critics attribute to Gaudenzio Ferrari.

The church of San Croce founded in 1080, originally built outside the town walls, under the patronage of Pope Gregorius VII, and re-built inside, based on designs by Pellegrino Tibaldi.

San Albino

During the Middle Ages, San Albino was a compulsory halting-place for via Francigena pilgrims and still is today. Just outside Mortara, this is one of the Christian mother-churches of the 5th century Lomellina, and was re-used by Charlemagne as a burial ground for soldiers falling in the battle between the Longobard and Frank armies.

The architectural style is developed from a blend of the Romanic and Renaissance styles. Against the Southern side of the porch there is a building, perhaps part of the ancient monastery. Beside the church, the cloister ruins are an open brick gallery with wooden architraves and a 14th century Gothic window decorated with rural motifs. Inside, on the right wall, there are three frescoes painted by Giovanni da Milan, representing Abbott St. Anthony, The Baptism of Jesus and Sitting on the Throne. Another fresco, by an unknown painter working during the first half of the 15th century, can be seen under the triptych and represents St. Laurent with the symbol of his martyrdom in his hand. Next to this fresco, there are some visible marks carved in the bricks by the pilgrims to remember their passage. The most ancient readable date is the year 1100.

Tromello XLII Tremel

Garlasco

Probably of pre-Roman origin, Garlasco was later donated, in the 10th century, to the monastery of San Salvatore di Pavia, at that time one of the greatest landowners in the area.

Of particular interest:

The church of Santa Maria Assunta is built in Corinthian style, with three naves and a magnificent dome built additionally in 1715 over the remains of the primitive church of Santa Maria, traces of which remain in the base of the tower and in the 15th century paintings in the apse.

Of particular interest is the beautiful marble pulpit adorned with bas-reliefs representing the Primacy of Peter, Jesus in the temple and the preaching of John the Baptist. On the opposite side is the organ, built in 1896 by the brothers Lingiardi, renowned builders of Pavia. The church of San Rocco was built on the back of Santa Maria Assunta by Count Giovanni Castiglioni in 1570. This contains treasures looted by Napoleon's troops in 1813.

The alternative route will take you through Madonna delle Bozzola, built around the Shrine of Our Lady of Bozzola, which dates back to a miraculous event in 1465. It was the first Sunday of September and a

thirteen-year-old deaf-mute girl, Mary of Garlasco, was grazing her animals when suddenly a thunderstorm broke. Mary sought shelter in a small chapel where there was a fresco of the Blessed Virgin Mary, painted by Augustine of Pavia, as a votive offering for being saved from drowning in the river Ticino. Suddenly a ball of light appeared and the Blessed Virgin Mary spoke, entrusting the girl with a mission: "*Here at Garlasco I want a sanctuary to protect the whole of Lomellina. Many are the graces that I pour into this place and my children will experience the treasures of my mercy.*" Maria returned to Garlasco and neighbours, hearing the child speak for the first time, believed her story. The sanctuary was indeed built, Mary was renamed Maria Benedett, and she subsequently withdrew to a convent nearby.

Pavia XLI Pamphica

The city stretches along the right bank of the Ticino River, and is dominated by Medieval towers which testify to the artistic and

architectural treasures waiting to be discovered. A vibrant and multi-faceted town with a great love of art and culture, there will be art exhibitions and other cultural events for you to enjoy, if you want to take a day off. The monuments, cobbled streets and house facades in the heart of Pavia's historical centre are strong reminders of its glorious past. Dating back to pre-Roman times, the town of Pavia (then known as *Ticinum*), was a municipality and an important military site under the Roman Empire. Later the city became known as *Papia* (probably as a reference to the Pope), which evolved to the Italian name Pavia. During Pavia's golden age, the city was the Lombard's capital and later witnessed coronations of Charlemagne and Frederick Barbarossa. Even after it lost its status to Milan in 1359, Pavia remained an important city and great Romanesque churches, tall towers and other monuments still reflect this.

Of particular interest:

The construction of Pavia's cathedral was an extremely long process, spanning over four centuries. Many people contributed to the design, including Leonardo Da Vinci, who visited Pavia during the early stages of the cathedral's construction. The church was not fully completed until the 1930s, more than four hundred years after the first stone was laid. The plan is a Greek cross, with three naves flanked by semi-circular chapels. The central nave is twice as wide as those on the side and divided by two galleries. The centre dome has an octagonal plan and is the fourth largest in Italy. The remains of St. Siro are conserved in the crypt, while the church also contains many other relics and, perhaps most importantly, a precious silver and crystal 17th century reliquary with the Holy Thorns of the Crown of Christ.

San Michele Maggiore is an outstanding example of Lombard-Romanesque church architecture, located on the site of a pre-existing Lombard church. Destroyed in 1004, the church was rebuilt from around the end of the 11th century (including the crypt, the transept and the choir) and finished in 1155. Emperor Frederick Barbarossa was crowned here.

San Pietro in Ciel d'Oro is the burial site of Saint Augustine, Boethius and the Lombard king Liutprand. The arch, which holds the relics of St. Augustine was built in 1362 by artists from Campione and is decorated by some one hundred and fifty statues and reliefs. The church is mentioned by Dante Alighieri in the X canto of his Divine Comedy.

San Teodoro, dedicated to Theodore of Pavia, a Medieval bishop of the Diocese of Pavia, is situated on the slopes leading down to the Ticino river and built to serve the fishermen. Inside, are two outstanding bird's-eye view frescoes of the city (1525) attributed to the painter Bernardino Lanzani.

Castello Visconteo (1360-1365), built by Galeazzo II Visconti was actually used as a private residence. The poet Francesco Petrarca spent some time there, when Gian Galeazzo Visconti called him to take charge of the magnificent library (over a thousand books and manuscripts), which was subsequently lost. The Castle is now home to the Musei Civici.

Santa Maria del Carmine, one of the best known examples of Gothic brickwork architecture in northern Italy and second largest church in the city.

The University of Pavia, founded in 1361, is one of the most ancient universities in Europe. The Medieval towers still shape the town's skyline. The main clusters are situated in Piazza Leonardo da Vinci, via Luigi Porta and Piazza Collegio Borromeo.

And finally, a definite highlight, and almost impossible to miss,

the Ticino bridge. This covered bridge is one of Pavia's most symbolic monuments, connecting the historical centre of the city to the area known as Borgo Ticino, a quarter once inhabited by washerwomen, fishermen and boatmen. The current bridge was constructed between the end of the 40s and the beginning of the 50s of the 20th century, following the destruction of the Medieval covered bridge, which was badly damaged during the Second World War. Unlike the current bridge, the old bridge had seven arches and towers with drawbridges at its extremities. A few ruins can still be seen further upstream.

Sante Cristina XL Sce Cristine

The history of Sante Cristine is linked to the old Benedictine abbey of the same name. Founded by Liuthprand, the King of the Lombards, the monastery was dedicated to St. Christine in the 9th century. In 1513 the Vallumbrosan monks replaced the Benedictine order in the monastery until its closure in 1654. As a point of interest Conradin, Duke of Swabia was given hospitality there in 1267, on his way across Lombardy to move against Charles I of Anjou.

Orio-Litta

Your first steps out of Orio-Litta will take you past the impressive Villa Litta Carini, an ancient noble villa dating back to the second half of the 17th century and built by Count Antonio Cavazzi of Somaglia who entrusted the work to architect Giovanni Ruggeri. Today the villa is used for events, but it does host a permanent antiques exhibition on two floors of the central part of the building.

Emilia-Romagna

Regione Emilia-Romagna

You will be crossing Emilia-Romagna, a broad corridor through the hills and plains of the Po Valley and the hot, Mediterranean south. With its rich agricultural land, historical cities and thriving industry, it is one of the most prosperous areas in Italy. Most of the major towns in Emilia-Romagna lie near the via Aemilia, a Roman road built in 187 BC, which linked Rimini on the Adriatic coast with the garrison town of Piacenza. Prior to the Romans, the Etruscans had ruled from their capital, *Felsina*, located on the site of present-day Bologna. After the fall of Rome, the region's focus moved to Ravenna, which became a principal part of the Byzantine Empire administered from Constantinople.

Today, the region is probably best known for being home to Ferrari, Lamborghini and Maserati, but it also has a reputation as a great gastronomic centre. Piacenza and its province are renowned for the production of seasoned and salted pork products. The main specialties being *pancetta* (rolled seasoned pork belly), *coppa* (seasoned pork neck) and *salame* (chopped pork meat flavoured with spices and wine and made into sausages). *Bortellina* (salted pancakes) and *chisulén* (flour, milk and animal fats mixed together and then fried) are also good with a cream cheese, particularly Gorgonzola and Robiola. The hills surrounding Piacenza are well known for their vineyards. The wine produced in this area is qualified with a D.O.C (Denominazione di origine controllata) called *Colli piacentini* (Hills of Piacenza). Main wines are Gutturnio (red wine, both sparkling and still), Bonarda (a red wine, often sparkling and foamy, made from Croatina grapes), Ortrugo (a dry white wine) and Malvasia (a sweet white wine).

Piacenza XXXVIII Placentia

Piacenza and Cremona were founded as Roman military colonies in 218 BC. Although sacked and devastated several times, the city always recovered and by the 6th century, Procopius was calling it "the principal city in the country of Aemilia".

The first Bishop of Piacenza (322–357), San Vittorio, declared Saint Antoninus of Piacenza, a soldier of the Theban Legion, the patron saint of Piacenza, and had the first basilica constructed in his honour in 324. The basilica was restored in 903, rebuilt in 1101, again in 1562, and is still a church today. The remains of the bishop and the soldier-saint are in urns under the altar. The theme of Antoninus, protector of Piacenza, is well known in art.

By the 16th century a coin featured the motto: *Placentia floret* (Piacenza flourishes) as testimony to the city's progress economically, chiefly due to the expansion of agriculture in the surrounding countryside.

Piacenza was ruled by France until 1521, and briefly, under Pope Leo X, as a member of the Papal States. In 1545, it became part of the newly created Duchy of Parma, ruled by the House of Farnese. In 1802, Napoleon's army annexed Piacenza to the French Empire and young Piacentini recruits were sent to fight in Russia, Spain and Germany, while the city was plundered of a great number of artworks, which are currently exhibited in many French museums. The Habsburg government of Marie Louise, Duchess of Parma (1816–1847), is remembered fondly as one of the best in the history of Piacenza. The duchess drained land, built several bridges and created educational and artistic activities. Finally, during World War II, the city was heavily bombed by the Allies. The important railway and road bridges across the Trebbia and the Po destroyed, and the historic centre of the city itself suffered considerable collateral damage.

Today, Piacenza is a quiet, provincial town, characterised by its historical monuments and other souvenirs of its rich past. It is also the headquarters of the European Association of The via Francigena.

Of particular interest:

Palazzo Farnese, commissioned by Ottavio's wife, Margaret of Austria, and built over a former fortress built by the Visconti in 1352, part of which can still be seen. In 1558, the architect Giacomo Barozzi da Vignola, produced drawings for a vast palace on a scale with the Vatican Palace, but the actual construction included less than half of his original project and lacked many of the planned architectural features. After the death of the last Farnese duke in 1731, the palace fell into disrepair and restoration only began in the early 20th century. Today, the Palazzo houses an important series of museums and exhibitions.

The Palazzo Communale, also known as *il Gotico*, (1281) is the seat of the government and one of the best preserved examples of the Medieval civic building in northern Italy known as the *Broletto.*

The Duomo di Piacenza is a Romanesque cathedral (1122 to 1233), housing frescoes made in the 14th-16th centuries by Camillo and Ludovico Carracci, Morazzone and Guercino. The main gate is decorated

with a large 15th century lunette, representing the Ecstasy of St. Francis. The interior, two aisles divided by low and strong brick pillars supporting high Gothic arches, has a Latin Cross scheme.

Piazza Cavalli, the main square of the town, is named after the two bronze equestrian monuments of Alessandro Farnese (Duke of Parma and Piacenza from 1586, nephew and valiant general of Philip II of Spain), and his son Ranuccio, who succeeded him to the dukedom.

The basilica of Sant'Antonino, an example of Romanesque architecture, is characterised by a large octagonal tower.

The basilica of San Savino, dedicated to St. Victor's successor, was begun in 903 but only consecrated in 1107. The façade and the portico are from the 17th-18th centuries.

The Bronze Liver of Piacenza, an Etruscan bronze model of a sheep's liver housed in Piacenza's Archaeological Museum (part of the Musei Civici di Palazzo Farnese), contains writing on its surface delineating the various parts of the liver and their significance. It was probably used as an educational tool for students studying haruspicy, or divination.

The Ricci Oddi Gallery is dedicated to modern Italian painters and a must for all art lovers.

Saint Antoninus of Piacenza

Saint Antonious, also known as Placentia, died 303 AD and is patron saint of Piacenza. He is venerated as a saint and martyr in the Roman Catholic Church, and said to have been martyred in either Piacenza or Travo, in the 303 AD Diocletianic Persecution. He appears in Victricius' *De Laude Sanctorum* of the same century, and then somewhat later in the *Martyrologium Hieronymianum*. Sabinus of Piacenza established his sanctuary, following a rediscovery of the relics. A later tradition made him a member of the legendary Theban Legion. Piacenza's Basilica di Sant'Antonino bears his name.

St. Rocco

Born of noble parentage in 1340 AD in Montpellier, France, San Rocco had a red, cross-shaped birthmark on the left side of his chest and, as a young child, showed great devotion to God. As an adult, he dressed in the clothes of a pilgrim and departed for Rome. Along the way, he stopped at Aquapendente, which was stricken by the plague, and devoted himself to the plague victims, curing them with prayer and the sign of the cross. He next visited Cesena and other neighbouring cities, and then finally Rome. Legend has it that everywhere he visited, the terrible scourge disappeared before his miraculous power, though while ministering in Piacenza he finally fell ill. As a result, Rocco was banished from the city and took refuge in a cave where he slept on leaves and drank water from a small stream. Miraculously, a dog is said to have brought him bread as a means of sustenance. The dog belonged to a lord, who lived nearby, and followed his hound to the woods where he discovered Rocco, took pity on him and gave him the medical care he needed. St. Rocco subsequently travelled through northern Italy to Rome, before returning to his birthplace in France. On arriving he was so weak and sick that the townspeople did not recognize him and threw him into jail as a spy, where he remained for five years until his death. Saint Rocco is venerated in the Roman Catholic Church as the protector against the plague and all contagious diseases. The statue of Saint Rocco is considered unique, because it depicts him with his left hand pointing to an open sore on his left leg. Few images of saints expose any afflictions or handicaps.

Saint Conrad

The saint's date of birth is uncertain, but it is known that he belonged to one of the noblest families of Piacenza. Having married when he was quite young, he then led a virtuous and God-fearing life until one day, while he was hunting in brushwood, he accidentally started a fire. The prevailing wind caused the flames to spread rapidly and the surrounding forest was soon engulfed. A mendicant, who happened to be near the place where the fire had originated, was accused of being the source, imprisoned, then tried and condemned to death. As the poor man was being led to his execution, Conrad, stricken with remorse, confessed his guilt and in order to repair the damage, sold all of his possessions. Reduced to poverty, Conrad retired to a lonely hermitage some distance from Piacenza, while his wife entered the Order of Poor Clares. Later, he went to Rome and then to Sicily, where for thirty years he lived a most austere life and worked numerous miracles until he died in 1351. Though bearing the title of saint, Conrad was never formally canonized.

The road from Piacenza to Fiorenzuola d'Arda takes you through flat, but infinitely interesting landscape. This swathe of the region of Emilia-Romagna is perhaps the richest in terms of its agriculture, with the countryside providing an abundant harvest and many of the regional food staples - Parma ham, salami and mortadella, as well as the emblematic *Parmigiano-Reggiano* (Parmesan cheese). Though the large farm houses and smaller churches you pass will not be notable historically, they are certainly worth pausing for and appreciating. This a pleasant section of the route.

Fiorenzuola d'Arda XXXVII Floricum

An attractive stopping place, this little town's name is derived from *Florentia*, meaning prosperous and d'Arda, which refers to the River Arda flowing from the Apennine Mountains into the valley, where Fiorenzuola is situated. It is also claimed the name could have been chosen in honour of Fiorenzo of Tours, who was said to have performed a miracle there while on his way to Rome in the 6th century. Fiorenzuola d'Arda was the most important stopping place for pilgrims, after Piacenza. Towards the end of the 11th century, King of Denmark, Henry I Svendsson, established a hospital there. Records also note the presence of a monastic institution entrusted to Tommaso, bishop of Piacenza.

Of particular interest:

The Collegiata of San Fiorenzo, a Gothic style, Roman Catholic collegiate, now parish church, built on the site of a church originally dedicated to St. Boniface in 824. The Romanesque crypt still maintains an altar dedicated to her. Today, the apse, presbytery and nave have frescoes mainly focused on the Life of San Fiorenzo by 15th century artists. The central pilaster have fragments of frescoes depicting the Madonna from 1520 and earlier. The ciborium dates from the late 11th-century.

Fidenza

For a considerable number of years, Fidenza was known as *Borgo San Donninore* (in honour of Saint Domninus), but it was renamed Fidenza in 1927, recalling its Roman name of *Fidentia*. In Roman times, the town was an important staging point on the via Emilia, but during the Middle Ages it was almost completely abandoned, until the remains of St Donnino were rediscovered in a grave on the eastern bank of the river Stirone. This was followed by a series of other miracles - the healing of a sick man, the location of a stolen horse, and the preservation of a number of believers when the bridge collapsed. The town has suffered destruction at the hands of the troops of Parma and, most recently, the Allies during the Second World War, but has been carefully restored and developed.

Of particular interest:

Fidenza Cathedral, constructed in the 12th century, was dedicated to Saint Domninus. The saint's relics were brought to Fidenza in 1207, and are believed to be contained in an urn in the crypt. The cathedral is an example of the Lombard-Romanesque style. The upper part of the façade is incomplete, but the lower, with its three portals and sculptures, is a fine example of Romanesque architecture, including two statues by Benedetto Antelami and bas-reliefs depicting the Histories of St. Domninus. The interior is simple and well-proportioned, and has not been spoilt by restoration. The statue of the apostle Simon Peter, at the front of the cathedral, is famous for its pointing in the direction of Rome.

While the cathedral is the main highlight in Fidenza, it's worth stopping off for Porta san Donnino, one of the Medieval gates that originally allowed access to the historical town. Similarly, the church of San Michelle, an 18th century neoclassical style, rebuilt over a much older church, is architecturally interesting.

Finally, spare a moment for the 12th century Palazza Communale (Town Hall), which was substantially rebuilt in the 14th and 16th centuries and had a new facade added in the 19th century.

Saint Domninus of Fidenza

Legend states that Domninus was Chamberlain to Emperor Maximian and keeper of the royal crown, until he converted to Christianity and incurred the emperor's wrath. Pursued by imperial forces, he rode through Piacenza holding a cross. He was caught and beheaded on the banks of the Stirone, outside Fidenza, after which he is supposed to have picked up his severed head and placed it on the future site of the cathedral of San Donnino. He died in 304 AD.

Walking out of Fidenza, you'll notice a tiny chapel dedicated to Thomas Beckett, the archbishop of Canterbury, martyred in 1170, by Henry II of England. The church was originally a chapel belonging to a Templar farmhouse. The apse dates back to the 12th century, and the extension of the aisle and arcade were built in the first half of the 15th. In the apse, you'll see three small splayed windows. The central window was reopened in 1954 and, during these restoration works, a frescoed fascia dating back to the first half of 400 AD was discovered. The frescoes represent the Trinity, Archangel Gabriel, the Crucifixion and St John the Baptist. The Trinity is represented with three identical figures who are going to eat, following a scheme that dates back to the biblical episode of the Lord who visits Abraham in the desert, very common in Byzantine culture, but rare in Western culture.

Thomas Becket

Born in around 1120, Beckett was the son of a prosperous London merchant. He was well educated and quickly became an agent to Theobald, Archbishop of Canterbury, who sent him on several missions to Rome. Becket's talents were noticed by Henry II, who made him his chancellor. The two became close friends. When Theobald died in 1161, Henry made Becket archbishop, after which Becket transformed himself from a pleasure-loving courtier into a serious, simply-dressed cleric.

The king and his archbishop's friendship was put under strain when it became clear that Becket would stand up for the church in its disagreements with the king. In 1164, realising the extent of Henry's displeasure, Becket fled to France, and remained in exile for several years. He returned in 1170.

On the 29 December 1170, four knights, believing the king wanted Becket out of the way, confronted and murdered him in Canterbury Cathedral. Becket was made a saint in 1173 and his shrine in Canterbury Cathedral became an important focus for pilgrimage.

Medesano XXXV Metane

The first record of the stage post in Medesano dates back to 805 when Iacopo, Bishop of Lucca, bought some lands in the Medesano region from Gariperto of Parma. Five years later, the same Bishop bought two other lots of land from a local inhabitant. The interest shown in the area by the bishops of Lucca was continued through to Bishop Pietro in 831, and is a demonstration of the way in which the church established its presence along the via Francigena. Medesano appears again as a key town in the 11th century, when the Emperor Henry II, entrusted his possessions to the Monastery of Leno, including those in Medesano.

Fornovo di Taro XXXIV Philemangenur

In Roman times, Fornovo di Taro was an important roadway settlement on the Parma-Lucca road, a market town known as *Forum Novum* and perhaps also a place of worship on the east bank of the Taro River. In the Middle Ages, the traffic - pilgrims, merchants and brigands - joined together

to climb up to the pass and find a resting place. The church of Santa Maria Assunta incorporates the statue of a pilgrim in its façade, indicating the direction of the route as a permanent sign. The original plan of the church, dating back to the 9th century, was rebuilt in the 11th century and then again in the 12th century, but this time with three naves, where the stone columns supported a trussed roof. In the 12th century a double-columned narthex (the entrance or lobby area, located at the end of the nave) was added to accommodate the increasing numbers of pilgrims who were arriving. In addition, the church was embellished with sculptures created by apprentices of the Antelame school. Fornovo di Taro is especially remembered as the site of the Battle of Fornovo, fought in 1495 between the Italian league and the French troops of Charles VIII.

Cisa Pass

The pass runs along the border between the Duchy of Parma and the grand Duchy of Tuscany, while also offering stunning views. Dominated by the chapel of Nostra Signora della Guardia, built in 1921, the pass is part of the via Francigena, but also one of the favourite itineraries followed by motorbike lovers in the province of Parma. At the top of the pass, in San Giorgio di Filattiera, a memorial tablet records the existence of a hospital for pilgrims dedicated to the Virgin Mary. Such was the importance of the pass that Parma's town council decreed that whoever went to live near the church should be tax exempt, the idea being to encourage the population of the pass and thereby make it safer. *"If no one goes there of their accord,"* the decree continues, *"it will rest with the men of Berceto, Valbona, Corchia*

and Bergotto to send groups of men in shifts throughout the month of May to secure the pass." In 1271 the revised version of the same decree prescribed the reconstitution and fortification of the hospice for the care of the people of Berceto. In 1471 the hospital was aggregated to the Ospedale Rodolfo Tanzi of Parma, but the chapel was later abandoned with disastrous consequences for the safety of the pass. In 1584, the Duke of Parma and the town of Pontremoli came to an agreement to ensure the presence of soldiers for six months of the year to protect the defenceless pilgrim, a guard that was still in operation in the 18th century.

Close by the Passo della Cisa, at the end of a steep staircase, there is a church dedicated to Our Lady of the Guard. Begun in 1919, it was consecrated on July 16, 1922 and declared a sanctuary on August 29, 1930. Since then, every August 29, the day dedicated to Our Lady of the Guard, believers make their pilgrimage to the church.

Tuscany

Renowned for its art, history and evocative landscape, with hill towns encircled by Etruscan walls and slender cypress trees, Tuscany is a region where the past and present merge in pleasant harmony. But even without these, the landscape - rolling hills so soft and continuous that this writer has the sense of walking over a recently petrified sea - is enough to make one want to add at least another week to the schedule. Tuscany must be seen at leisure and preferably on foot. Like all of Italy, Tuscany has its Etruscan and Roman past, with the scars and treasures associated with each. Today, as you walk through the countryside, among the vineyards and olive groves, you will encounter hamlets and farmhouses, as well as fortified villas and castles, symbolizing the violence and inter-communal strife that tore Tuscany apart during the Middle Ages. Several imposing castles and villas were built for the Medici family, the great patrons of the Renaissance, who supported eminent scientists, such as Galileo. Northern Tuscany and the heavily populated plain between Florence and Lucca, which the via Francigena

will take you through, is dominated by industry, with intensively cultivated land between the cities and the wild mountainous areas. At the heart of central Tuscany lies Siena, also on your route, which was involved in a long feud with Florence. Its finest hour came with its victory in the Battle of Montaperti in 1260, but the town was devastated by the Black Death in the 14th century, and finally suffered a crushing defeat in the siege of 1554-5.

North-eastern Tuscany, with its mountain peaks and woodland, provided refuge for hermits and saints, while the east was home to Piero della Farncesca, the early Renaissance painter. Along with its great artists, Tuscany is also known for its famous writers and poets, most notably Florentine author Dante. Tuscany's literary scene thrived in the 13th century and the Renaissance.

Along with the culture there is the landscape and the food it provides. Olive groves and wild herbs grow everywhere. Many of the best oils are reserved for use as a condiment at the table, rather than as an ingredient. Tuscan cooking has its roots in *cucina povera* (peasant cooking) and is indeed very simple. No fancy sauces, no elaborate creations or heavy seasoning. Meat and fish tends to be grilled simply over a fire, vegetables served raw, steamed or sautéed. Pasta plays a small role in the diet, but certainly not as much as it does in other parts of Italy, because salads and a variety of bean dishes, predominate.

Tuscany is home to some of the world's most notable wine regions. Chianti, Brunello di Montalcino and Vino Nobile di Montepulciano are primarily made with Sangiovese grape, whereas the Vernaccia grape is the basis of the white Vernaccia di San Gimignano. Tuscany is also known for the dessert wine Vin Santo, made from a variety of the region's grapes. In the 1970s a new class of wines known in the trade as "Super Tuscans" emerged. These wines were made outside DOC/DOCG regulations, but were considered of high quality and commanded high prices. Many have become cult wines.

Pontremoli   XXXI Puntremel

Contested since its origin, this little town has been split between the regions of Parma, Liguria and Tuscany so many times that it has acquired a quite unique personality, dialect and charm, Set on a strip of land between the two converging waterways, the rivers Magra and Verde, this little town has been burned to the ground, destroyed and conquered, only to rise time and time again.

The focus for all this combative activity was the settlement's singular position, which opened roads not only east-west but also north-south, with a continuous parade of pilgrims searching for the Holy Land and Rome, attested by the number of hospitals built within the town or nearby – including Ospedale dei Santi Giacomo e Leonardo and the church of San Pietro run by the monks of Altopascio.

Pontremoli is believed to have been settled around a thousand years before Christ and was called *Apua* by the Romans. Medieval in plan, the town is dominated by the imposing mass of the Piagnoro castle, high above the rest of the town that spreads along the banks of the Magra. Literally translated, Pontremoli means Trembling Bridge (from the Italian *tremare* - to tremble), named after a prominent bridge across the Magra, which, one presumes, trembled.

If you happen to be in Pontremoli in January, you could experience one of the more exciting traditions of the town, where the two competing *rioni* (districts) stage a bonfire in honour of San Geminiano, under the arches of the Ponte della Cesa. The winner is the *rioni* that presents not only the highest flames, but also the most beautiful fire.

Of particular interest:

Pontremoli Cathedral is dedicated to the Virgin Mary, as thanks for her ending the plague of 1622. The present church was erected between 1636 and 1687 using designs by the architect Alessandro Capra.

La Torre del Cacciaguerra, also known as the *Campanone*, was built in 1322 to keep guard over the two warring factions in the small town. The tower, aptly named *looking for a fight*, is located between the Square of the Cathedral and the Square of the Repubblica.

The Chapel of the Santissimo Sacramento and the façade also date to the 1800s (1828 and 1878-1881 respectively), the latter of which was designed by the Florentine Vincenzo Micheli, and built by the architects Giovanni Pacini and Pasquale Poccianti. The rich imagery inside the church can be considered a sort of anthology of 18th century painting. Amongst the works, there are important paintings depicting the Virgin Mary in the presbytery and the choir, including the Birth of the Virgin by Ferretti, the Visitation by Meucci, The Marriage of the Virgin by Peroni and the Annunciation by Giuseppe Bottani.

The church of San Pietro is just outside the historic centre, but is important because it hosts one of the principal symbols of the via Francigena – a labyrinth made of eleven circles. After being destroyed in World War II, the church was completely rebuilt and now displays this symbol of travelling towards God and metaphor of the difficulties one will have on the path of life - just like the perils of travelling along the via Francigena.

Ponte della Cresa, commonly known as Ponte di San Francesco di Sopra, spans the river Verde with four stone arches and was one of the principal entrances into the city when coming from the direction of Piacenza. Originally built of wood, this bridge dates back to the 1300's and has been rebuilt several times due to the flooding of the Verde River.

Piagnaro Castle was built in the 10th century to protect the citizens of Pontremoli, and is probably the first and original structure of the town. The etymology of the name Piagnaro, derives from *piagne*, meaning the sandstone slabs used to tile the roofs. The complex architecture of the Castle is the result of numerous reconstructions and enlargements, and is characterized by the imposing 15th century tower at the highest point of the Castle. In front of the tower, pilgrims are offered accommodation in what were the barracks for soldiers. A wonderful and evocative experience, much recommended by your author. How many of us can say that we had the castle to ourselves for the night? Since 1975, Piagnaro Castle has been host to the Museum of the Stele Statues of Lunigiana dedicated to Augusto Cesare Ambrosi. A must-see. The Stele Statues are enigmatic stone sculptures dating between 4 and 1 thousand AD, and this exhibition is the most important collection of sculptures from prehistoric Europe.

Stele statues

Present in many European cultures, from Central and Eastern Europe, as well as in Corsica and Sardinia, Italy's oldest stele statues are found in the border areas between Liguria and Tuscany, as well as in northern Puglia. Their locations suggesting sacred areas outside both settlements areas and necropoli.

The statues, though they all bear the resemblance which enables them to be identified as Stele, can actually be divided into three groups.

Group A, the oldest, have highly stylized anthropomorphic features. The head an extension of the body, with a typical U shape, with the arms as simple bas-reliefs and the fingers rarely present. The males are identified by a dagger with a triangular blade, a short handle and a semi-circular knob, while the females are represented with separate breasts, stylised as small disks.

Group B corresponds to an intermediate period, and presents greater detail. The defining characteristic is the shape of the head, separated from the body by a cylindrical neck. The neck may still be U-shaped, but other details such as the eyes are now evident. The weapons of the male statues remain the traditional triangular daggers, but are more detailed and often include an L-shaped, long handle axe. The female statues have hemispherical breasts and sometimes stylised jewels.

Group C, the most recent group, is the most artistically evolved, but has only male stele statues. The figures are more realistic and include far more detail than groups A and B. The head is rounded, detached from the body, with well-defined facial features. The same for the hands and arms, with some details of the weapons and clothes.

Filetto

This small town dates back to the 6th and 7th centuries, a period of time when Byzantine populations required fortresses for defense against the Longobards.

The original town layout is a square defended by four cylindrical towers, one of which still stands today. The first town centre was later transformed into a fortified residence that underwent numerous renovations until the 17th century. The interior part of town, accessed by two monumental city gates houses a church dedicated to the saints Filippo and Giacomo.

Of particular interest:

The Palazzo of the Marquis Ariberti, an impressive 17th century building connected to the church by two elegant elevated passageways.

The Frati Ospitalieri Convent, a vast 17th century complex featuring a beautiful internal cloister.

The hospice of Selva Donica (now in ruins) in the Filetto forest, was established to support the pilgrims who passed through.

If you are passing through in August, you may be in time for the Filetto Medieval Market, with its jugglers, fortune tellers, minstrels, acrobats and traditional local artisanal products made of iron, wood and stone.

From here, the route continues through small villages and along canals until reaching Aulla. The territory of Castelnuovo Magra is crossed by a stretch of the Canale Lunense, a water system built in the 19th century. This area originally belonged to Luni, a Roman colony founded in the 2nd century BC.

Aulla XXX Aguilla

The name Aulla probably comes from the Latin words *lacus* or *lacuna*, meaning lake. Traces of Roman and Etruscan civilizations found in the

Church of Saint Caprisio indicate that there were settlements in Aulla long before the 8th century, when Adalberto of Tuscany founded a village and castle to accommodate pilgrims travelling the via Francigena. The church, dedicated to Santa Maria Assunta, has since undergone profound changes, but the primitive 10th century structure remains, along with the semi-circular apse and a fragment of stone carved with vegetal motifs. A museum has been created in the old rectory and contains items from the church's pilgrim past, but the whole presbytery area has been excavated and can be visited. In addition to the monumental tomb of the saint one can also see the ruins of a 7th century church, with an attractive marble floor made of Roman marble. During the Middle Ages, the Abbey became one of the most influential religious centres in the Lunigiana region and in 1522 the village of Aulla was bought by the commander Giovanni delle Bande Nere, who built the imposing Fortress of Brunella. In 1943, the historic centre of Aulla was destroyed by Anglo-American bombings, aimed at German troups stationed there during the Second World War.

Of particular interest:

The fortress of Brunella - a splendid example of military architecture dating back to the first half of the 16th century. Built with the same brown volcanic rock on which it is built.

Santo Stefano di Magra *XXIX Sce Stephane*

Located near the confluence of the Vara with the Magra river, Santo Stefano di Magra is in the Montemarcello-Magra Natural Regional Park. Founded before 1000 AD, the settlement was described as a marketplace in 981 by Emperor Otto II and in 1185 by Emperor Frederick. Today, the town is divided into two parts by the old central road and enclosed by powerful late Renaissance walls. The church, dedicated to St. Stephen, was built in the 18th century over a Medieval pieve (a term defining rural churches with a baptistery).

Sarzana

The first mention of the city is found in 983, but owing to its militarily strategic position, it changed masters more than once, belonging first to Pisa, then to Florence, then to the Banco di San Giorgio of Genoa and from 1572 to Genoa itself. The town is based around the via Francigena that passes between the city gates of Parma and Romana, but is also known as a centre for trade in antiques.

Of particular interest:

The Firmafede Fortress was built in the second half of the 15th century on the ashes of the former 13th century Pisan fortification. It represents an important example of Florentine military architecture of the end of the 15th century. With the annexation of the republic to the kingdom of Savoy, and the radical changes of defensive strategies, the fortress was first used as a police station and later as a prison until the 1970s. Between 1985 and 2003, a series of restorations have made the Fortress usable once again, and it is now used for many cultural activities, which make visits to the interior difficult. Nevertheless, seen from the outside it is an impressive, almost overwhelming, presence.

Of particular interest:

The cathedral, Santa Maria Assunta di Sarzana is a mixture of Romanesque and Gothic styles, reflecting the length of the period of its construction, from the early 13th to the late 15th century. The west front is white marble, featuring a portal with a small Gothic rose window above it, between two side blocks. The campanile, at the south side is the only remaining part of the previous Pieve di San Basilio. The ground plan is in the form of a Latin cross, while the nave is divided into three aisles by two arcades of widely spaced polygonal columns supporting high arches. The cathedral houses a relic of the Blood of Christ, and the important Romanesque Cross of Maestro Guglielmo of 1138, the oldest known painted Italian crucifix.

Luni XXVIII Luna

The Roman city of *Luna* was established in 177 BC, as a military stronghold for the campaigns against the Ligures. There are different theories regarding the origins of the town's name. Some believe it was named after the ancient goddess Lunae, while others claim the name was inspired by the shape of its territory and harbour, which resembled a crescent moon (luna).

Luni derived its importance from its harbour, which was on a gulf of the Tyrrhenian Sea, now known as the Gulf of La Spezia. The site was used as a base for quarrying marble from the quarries of modern-day Carrara, after which it was shipped directly to Rome.

The spreading of malaria in the area and the silting up of the port contributed to the settlement's steep decline, and in 1058 the whole population moved to Sarzana, while other refugees went on to found Ortonovo and Nicola.

Luni was excavated in the 1970s and the artefacts are now housed in the adjacent museum. Archaeological evidence suggests that the Roman forum had been abandoned as a public space by the end of the 6th century, its buildings fell to ruin or were demolished and decorative marbles removed. Today's via Francigena route offers a short cut directly through Luni, and so a wonderful opportunity to visit the archaeological site.

Avenza

The name originates from the river it was built next to, the Aventia. The region flourished thanks to its optimal position along the ancient Via Aemilia Scauri (then called ' Romea' or 'Francigena '), and nearby Tyrrheanian Sea, which made it an excellent centre for the export of marble. In the 13th century, Avenza was encircled by fortified walls and its military strategic importance grew. The castle, built leaning against the city walls, was strengthened in the 14th century by Castruccio Castracani, Lord of Lucca. In the second half of 1500, Alberico Cybo Malaspina drained the surrounding plain and restructured all the fortifications. In 1848 the inhabitants of Avenza tried to get independence from the commune of Carrara, many times, but always without success.

After the unity of Italy, the fortress was sold to a private individual for use as a stone quarry, and only the intervention of the German historian Theodor Momsen, in 1883, saved it from total destruction. In 1859 the opening of a new road separated the fortress from the other main part of the castle-complex, the so called *Casino del Principe*, a 16th century fortified manor joined together with one of the angle towers of the town walls. It still exists today, though radically altered, and with little of the original building visible. Other remnants of the fortifications can be seen in the town-walls.

Of particular interest:

The local Church of St Peter in Avenza, was built in 1187, and rebuilt in the early 17th century in piazza Mazzini, named after Giuseppe Mazzini whose statue was erected there in 1913. The church is built according to Medieval design. The arms of Luni are still visible on the counter-facade, indicating that the church belonged to that town until the 12th century.

The Ospital di Sant'Antonio, a building that used to offer pilgrim accommodation, was closed at the end of 18th century and replaced by one of the 19th century aisles of the church. Today, a small hostel has been re-established next to the church for via Francigena pilgrims. The church is best-known for a wooden cross, thought to bring about miracles and provide strength.

Massa

From Avenza, the route winds through the area of Carrara, most famous for its white marble from which Michelangelo sculptured his David. All around you will see that the mountains have white peaks where the slopes have been opened and emptied of their precious marble interiors.

Massa, is the capital of the province of Massa-Carrara. Though not as well-known as its Carrara counterpart, the city is a real treasure chest of artistic and architectural gems. If you have a day spare, spend it here. According to historical documents, Massa dates from 882, and became a Medieval urban centre in the 11th and 12th centuries, while from the 15th to 19th centuries, it was the capital of the independent Principate of Massa and Carrara, ruled by the Malaspina and Cybo-Malaspina families, who were responsible for its significant development both culturally and economically.

Of particular interest:

Malaspina Castle crowns the top of a rocky hill, and dominates the wide underlying plain and part of the Tyrrhenian coast. It is not on the route, but will nevertheless be very present. From the 17th century the main purpose of the castle was military and served as a prison until 1946. Since then, the castle has been restored and opened to the public. Malaspina was visited by Dante Alighieri, who supposedly envisioned the descending circles of Hell there, and inspired the corresponding part in his Divine Comedy. According to legend, Dante saw the great funnel-shaped cave lying below, surrounded by a series of ledges with the slopes converging to the stream.

Massa cathedral, was built on the remains of the previous San Francesco monastery and consecrated in 1389. However, it only became a cathedral in the early 1800s, when the old cathedral, in piazza Aranci, was demolished on the order of Napoleon's sister, Elisa Baciocchi, then governess of the Lucca Republic. The façade is a 1936 reconstruction, based on designs by Cesario Fellini, while the basement holds the Cybo-Malaspina tomb, the final resting place of the town's princes. The interior consists of one single, spacious nave interrupted by a cross, with eight altars and the high altar of the apse, all richly ornate in multicoloured marble.

Piazza degli Aranci, decorated with a ring of orange trees, offers a break from the bustle of the city. This is the main piazza in Massa, designed by Élisa Baciocchi (daughter of Felice Baciocchi and Elisa Bonaparte), in order to give greater prominence to her Ducal Palace.

The Palazzo Ducale was begun by Alberico I Cybo Malaspina in 1567, but did not take definitive shape until the 18th century. When Napoleon added the Duchy of Massa and Carrara to the possessions of his sister Élisa in 1806. The princess decided to use the palazzo as her residence and for her court. The façade, is characterized by a potent contrast between the red of the plaster and the white of the stucco and marble decorations Inside, in the courtyard, a marble monumental stair leads to the Salone degli Svizzeri (the Salon of the Swiss), which is embellished with elegant decorative motifs, and the Salone degli Specchi (Salon of Mirrors). From the courtyard one also accesses the Nymphaeum, located between the Ducal Library and the Royal Stage. The rich Baroque decoration illustrates the deeds of the Cybo family. The Palazzo currently hosts a conference centre and exhibition spaces, and is the seat of the Province and of the Prefecture-Territorial Office of the Government of Massa Carrara.

Pietrasanta

Straddling the last foothills of the Apuan Alps, Pietrasanta has Roman origins and part of the Roman wall still exists. The Medieval town was founded in 1255 and built on the pre-existing Rocca di Sala fortress of the Lombards, by Luca Guiscardo da Pietrasanta. At its height, Pietrasanta was a part of the Genova citystate (1316 -1328). Then, in 1494, Charles VIII of France took control of the town, and it remained so, until Pope Leo X gave Pietrasanta back to the Medici family.

The town suffered a long period of decline during the 17th and 18th centuries, partially due to malaria, but in 1841, the Grand Duke of Tuscany, Leopold II di Lorena, promoted several reconstruction projects. He particularly focused on the building of schools to teach carving skills and the reopening of the once famous quarries, which brought back much of the town's former glory.

The urban plan of Pietrasanta is typical of foundation cities, rectangular in shape with a grid network of roads, the most important being the via Francigena, while the main transversal axis forms the square which the principal buildings face into. Pietrasanta grew in importance during the 15th century, mainly due to its connection with marble. Michelangelo was the first sculptor to recognize the beauty of the local stone. Today's artists and sculptors are drawn to Pietrasanta from all over the world. The Colombian painter and sculptor Fernando Botero as well as the Polish sculptor Igor Mitoraj, have residences in the commune.

Of particular interest:

The cathedral, Duomo di San Martino, dates back to the first half of the 14th century. From the front, the great rose window in the façade stands out, and the 15th century bell tower, by Donato Benti, is more than thirty metres high. The interior of the cathedral is also interesting, including some remarkable paintings by Pietro Dandini, and a late Gothic tableau depicting the 'Madonna and Saints'. The marble pulpit, is considered a masterpiece, with the high relief sculptures also attributed to Donato Benti. The bronze statues depicting angels are beautiful.

The Archaeology Museum of Versilia is inside the Palazzo Moroni and houses finds dating back to the Neolithic era, plus the Art Pottery of the Roman and Medieval Ages.

The Church of St. Augustine, dating from the 14th century, is a work of the Augustinian monks, who later also built the Monastery. The marble façade of the church is characterized by three large arches, surmounted by elegant Gothic arches supported by little columns. Particularly important from an artistic point of view is the first altar on the right, dating from the 15th century.

Proceeding to Via Mazzini, and towards the so-called Porta a Massa, you pass a number of civic and religious buildings, ranging from the Middle Ages and the Renaissance, until the 19th century. These include the Medieval Church of San Biagio, the Ponticelli Palace, the Albiani Palace and the Masini Palace.

The Bozzetti Sculpture Museum exhibits sketches, models and drawings of sculptures by hundreds of Italian and foreign artists, who have worked in Pietrasanta, including Botero, Cascella, Theimer, Folon, Mitoraj, Yasuda, Pomodoro, Tommasi and Gina Lollobrigida.

Between the 13th and 14th centuries, the via Francigena profoundly influenced the history of the Tuscan territories, giving shape and body to the regions it crossed. Right from the start this road, built by Longobards for linking the kingdom of Pavia with the dukedoms of Lucca and Beneveto, wound its way through the valleys of central Tuscany, avoiding the territories controlled by the Byzantines, and bringing with it a profound transformation in the road network. During the era of Charles the Great, it became the main connection between the peninsula and the area beyond the Alps, as well as the main axis of the Holy Roman Empire. From then on it was followed by pilgrims travelling to Rome, but also by kings and the ecclesiastical dignitaries, the most renowned being Sigeric, the Archbishop of Canterbury. The via Francigena leads us back into the Middle Ages in Tuscany, not only as a journey into the past, but also as a means of learning about its peculiarities and identity. Some areas it passed through, particularly those at the borders, were characterised by numerous fortified structures. Others, thanks to the growth of economic exchange, became centres of trade between the Orient and the West, from Alexandria in Egypt to the markets in the Champagne, France. The birth of the via Francigena gave new life to cities like Lucca and Sienna, and smaller settlements - San Miniato, San Gimignano, Colle Valdelsa and Pescia - all of them becoming leaders in the European Economy of the Middle Ages.

Camaiore XXVII Campmaior

Camaiore owes its origins to the Romans, who, after establishing Lucca, set up outposts on the slopes of Monte Prana. Among these was Camaiore, whose name comes from the ancient toponym *Campus Major,* the large plain that linked Lucca to the port in Luni. Later, this territory came under the dominion of the Lombards, followed by the feudal lords in Lucca, who re-established the town's original blueprint, beginning to transform it into the elegant Medieval town pilgrims go through now. The buildings in Camaiore's historic centre are a testament to its past.

Of particular interest:

The collegiate Church of Santa Maria Assunta, first mentioned in 1260, is located in the heart of Camaiore, and characterized by an austere asymmetric façade and the unique position of its bell tower in the left-hand nave. Particularly noteworthy are the grand rosette decorating the façade, and the precious 16th century decorative elements in the church's interior.

San Michele Arcangelo in Contesora

You could easily miss the little church on the roadside running through open fields and woodlands, but you should pause for a few minutes to appreciate its important history in terms of the pilgrimage to Rome. Right from the date of its founding by Ugolino in 1175, the Church of San Michele Arcangelo was attached to a hospice for pilgrims. The hospice itself was destroyed by German troops in 1944, but the church is still standing, even if it could do with some restoration and care.

Lucca XXVI Luca

Lucca was founded on the banks of the Serchio river, but its origins are the object of historical research and disagreement. On the one hand, some scholars claim that the Ligurians first set up in the area and that the name, Lucca, might therefore come from the Celtic-Ligurian word *Luk*, meaning marsh. On the other, researchers attribute the birth of the city to the Etruscans, according to recent archaeological finds. However, it is agreed by all that Lucca was colonised and developed by the Romans in 180 BC. The city still maintains the Roman orthogonal planning, which divided the space within the walls into regular blocks. In later years, Lucca became an independent republic as part of feudal Italy,

but was conquered by Napoleon and finally became part of Unified Italy in 1860. For the visitor today, Lucca is a fascinating city, packed full of monuments representing all the various historical epochs it has lived through, beginning with a Roman amphitheatre – today piazza dell'Anfiteatro – a circular space that has retained its original shape and sense of communal venue, thanks to its architect, Lorenzo Nottolini. Following this, there is the Medieval era, and perhaps what one could say are Lucca's true treasures. Its nickname, the city of one hundred churches, is not a random choice, because it does have a remarkable and vastly varied collection. So many, that your author has opted to discuss just two, and let you, the reader, discover as many others as you have the stamina and time for.

Having said that, the Medieval centre of Lucca is much more than just the sum of its churches, and a very welcome relief from the considerably less attractive suburbs you will have walked through to get there. The walls offer a perfect contrast. Surrounding the old centre, this defensive network was built during the Renaissance, and still stands to this day as one of the most complete and well preserved fortifications in Italy, some four kilometres in length.

For quiet resting and reflection, you can go to the beautiful Communal Botanical Gardens of Lucca, which cover two of the bastions on the city walls. Established in 1820, by the Duchess of Parma, the gardens feature a huge and beautiful variety of trees, plants and flowers.

Of particular interest:

Lucca cathedral is a place of legend and emotion, described as the jealous guardian of the Volto Santo, or Holy Countenance, it also houses the tomb of Ilaria del Carretto, one of the finest works of 15th century Italian sculpture. Located in Piazza San Martino, Cattedrale di San Martino is renowned for its stunning façade and design. Construction was begun during the 11th century, but the church was re-designed to be

in its current form during the 14th century Renaissance. The front façade features a series of opulent archways and an ornate portico framing the front doors. Look out for the vividly expressive equestrian sculpture (circa 1240), dedicated to the episode that changed the life of San Martino. Under the same arcade is a labyrinth carved in stone. Following a Chartres-type design, the labyrinth is cut into a single stone and acts as bas-relief. Similar to other Italian labyrinths, the one from Lucca draws parallels between the pagan Theseus and Christ. On the right-hand side, a Latin inscription reads: "*This is the labyrinth built by Dedalus of Crete, from which none could escape except Theseus helped by Ariadne's thread.*" The labyrinth once contained the images of Theseus and the Minotaur, but over hundreds of years, the fingers of thousands have gradually rubbed these characters out, so that today no trace of them remains. Next to the church is the half-finished, immense bell tower, its lower half of exposed brick creating a strong a contrast to the white walls of the top two levels. Inside, there is a plethora of beautiful artwork, one of the main features being the Sacred Face of Lucca, a venerated wooden body of a crucifix. Medieval legends say that it had been sculpted by Nicodemus, who assisted Joseph of Arimathea to place Christ in the tomb.

The Basilica di San Michele in Foro is another stunning church, which features a front façade unlike any other in the city. The original church was first mentioned in the 8th century, but gained its current form during the 13th century. Above the main arches of the façade are four rows of ornate arches and columns, which feature a number of different colours and designs. The level of detail is quite astounding from the carvings on the columns, to the stonework around the rose windows. The interior contains some important artworks by Luca della Robbia and Filippno Lippi.

The Puccini Museum is in the house where he was born. Visitors can walk through it and view all sorts of manuscripts, music scores, photos and even costumes from his operas. A wonderful way to discover more about this interesting Tuscan composer, and perhaps step back from the pilgrimage theme for a brief moment.

The Torre delle Ore has served as both a defensive fortification and a clock tower during its 700-year history. Created in the 14th century, the tower was part of a private structure and originally used for protection, but with time the need for defence lessened, so the Torre delle Ore was turned into a clock tower instead. Today you can climb to the top for incredible views of the city.

The Aqueduct of Nottolini dominates the skyline to the south of Lucca. A marvel of architectural and engineering achievement once used to carry water from the mountains into the city. Its four hundred arches made from stone stretch over three kilometres. Today the aqueduct still stands in its entirety and you can follow the structure from its beginning at the Temple cistern, through to its end at the Parco dell'Acquedotto.

San Martino

Legend has it that San Martino became a monk after serving as a Roman soldier. On a cold rainy day in November, Martino was traveling on horseback, and came across a poor beggar shivering from the cold. Martino took pity on him, and cut his own cloak in half, giving one half to the beggar. As soon as Martino set off again on his journey, the sun came out and the temperature became warm. From this we get the *Estate di San Martino* – the Summer of San Martino.

That night, Martino dreamt of Jesus wearing his cloak, and woke up with his own cloak intact. This sign prompted him to ask for baptism and become a Christian. Besides bringing warm November weather, San Martino has many chores as a patron saint of horseman, horses, tailors, beggars, the poor, injured, barrel makers, winemakers, drunks, cured alcoholics, and last but not least, betrayed husbands.

Giacomo Puccini

Puccini was born on December 22, 1858, in Lucca. He is best known for starting the operatic trend toward realism, with his popular works like La Bohème, Madame Butterfly and Tosca. His family had been tightly interwoven with the musical life of Lucca, providing five generations of organists and composers to the Cathedral of San Martino, so it was taken for granted that Giacomo would carry on this legacy. But the young Puccini was disinterested and a generally poor student, until he saw a production of Giuseppe Verdi's Aida, which changed his life.

Puccini's best known compositions would become the most widely performed in opera's history. As his fame spread, Puccini spent the next few years travelling the world to attend productions of his operas, to ensure they met his high standards. He would continue to work on new compositions as well, but his often complicated personal life saw to it that nothing remarkable was forthcoming for some time. Seeking to achieve his former glory in the face of fading popularity, Puccini set out to write his masterwork in 1920, throwing all of his hopes and energies into the project, which he titled Turandot, but his ambitions would never be fully realized. In 1923, Puccini complained of a recurring sore throat and sought medical advice. Though an initial consultation turned up nothing serious, during a subsequent examination he was diagnosed with throat cancer. As the cancer was, by that point, inoperable, Puccini travelled to Brussels in 1924 for an experimental radiation treatment. Too weak to endure the procedure, he died in the hospital seven days later, on November 29, 1924. At the time of his death, Puccini had become the most commercially successful opera composer of all time, worth the equivalent of an estimated $200 million,

Capannori

After leaving Lucca, you will pass the Athena Museum of Archeology and Ethnology in Capannori, which houses three main exhibitions: an archaeological display, an area dedicated to rural life and another highlighting the life of Carlo Piaggia, a local explorer. Pilgrims can also get a stamp for their passports here, but even more excitingly, the chance to walk through the *Labirinto del Pellegrino* or *Capannori Labyrinth*, a permanent wooden installation, which follows the shape of a scallop, the symbol of the Francigena route.

During the Middle Ages the territorial organisation of the Piana di Lucca was closely linked to the birth and growth of the Sei Miglia district. Emperor Enrico IV granted the city of Lucca important privileges for defending the commercial trade along the via Francigena, the river trade on the Serchio river and sea trade via the port of Motrone. He also banned the building of castles within a six mile radius of the city, thus establishing the borders of the city of Lucca's jurisdiction. Because of this, the district of Sei Miglia was established and some of the most important examples of Tuscan-Romanesque history are preserved in this area.

On your way out of the town you will pass the Church of Santi Quirico e Giulitta, Capannori. Originally called San Quirico a Quarto alla Rotta, it is mentioned in documents as early as 786. Unfortunately, it was destroyed in the 10th century, and rebuilt in the 12th century in the style now evident. The church has a single nave, with a facade notable for blind arches. The interior of the apse was frescoed in 1897 by Michele Marcucci, who also painted the Sacred Heart in the right transept and the Souls of Purgatory in the second altar on the right. The Polyptych of Santi Quirico e Giulitta (1448) painted by Borghese di Pietro Borghese were removed and are now on display in the Courtauld Institute.

Porcari   XXV Forcri

Leaving Lucca, the route goes through Porcari, a relatively unremarkable village today, but previously home to one of the greatest Italian families, the Porcari. In the Middle Ages the village was a stage on the via Francigena, and houses the Church of St. Justus, first built in the 16th century, but later mostly renovated in neo-Medieval style.

Altopascio

Altopascio has been known as a stopover for pilgrims on the via Francigena for centuries, but it is also called the "city of bread" because of the long-standing traditions passed down through generations in a region known for its abundance of grain.

In the historic centre, the Church of San Jacopo, built in 1100, during the great reign of the Order of Hospitallers is worth stopping for. The façade is decorated with smooth stone at the base and with horizontal stripes of white and green marble at the top. There is also a notable marble lunette above the doorway with two stone lions standing guard. The impressive bell tower was built in 1280 and its Medieval turrets can still be seen intact. The piazza dei Ospitalieri, the most significant square in the historic centre, has an interesting octagonal well at its centre. Here, the road passes near the monastery of Pozzeveri, which once stood on the banks of the now dried Lake Bientina, and whose church still preserves some Romanesque elements. Altopascio's hospital does not appear on Sigeric's itinerary, because it was founded (1084) after his pilgrimage. Nevertheless, it was an important institution because of its position on a particularly difficult section of road that passed between the marshes of Fucecchio and Bientina, an ideal place for brigands to attack the unprotected pilgrims. This formed the basis of the later Order of Saint James of Altopascio founded by Matilda of Canossa between 1070 and 1080. The town is also famous for the battle of Altopascio, in which the Ghibelline leader Castruccio Castracani defeated the Florentines Guelphs led by Ramon de Cardona. Thanks to his victory, he became duke of Lucca. During the 13th and 14th centuries, Altopascio's monastery had daughter houses in various parts of Italy and Europe, but began to decline because pilgrims were preferring to use other roads to Rome. The historical nucleus of Altopascio corresponds to the plan of a Medieval hospital. The three squares open out into as many courtyards, around which were distributed the functional buildings, but unfortunately since being converted into a farm and hamlet, little of the original architecture remains.

Matilda of Canossa

Matilda of Canossa, also known as Matilda the Great Countess, was born in Lucca, in 1046. The assassination of her father, Boniface of Canossa, and the deaths of her older brother and sister left her the sole surviving heir to the extensive holdings of the House of Attoni, founded by her grandfather Atto Adalbert. Two years later Matilda's mother, Beatrice, married Godfrey, duke of Upper Lorraine, an enemy of the emperor Henry III. Henry seized Beatrice and Matilda as hostages in 1055 and took them to Germany, but the following year he became reconciled with Godfrey and released them a few months before his own death.

When Godfrey died in 1069, Matilda married his son Godfrey the Hunchback, but after the death of their child in infancy, she returned to Italy, reigning with her mother until Beatrice's death in 1076. Matilda's father, for many years a supporter of the German emperors, had moved toward the papal side in the factional struggle dividing Italy, but Matilda remained loyal to the popes. She became a close friend of Pope Gregory VII, lending him important support in his struggle against the emperor Henry IV, and it was in her castle at Canossa that Gregory received the barefoot penance of the Emperor. After Henry's excommunication in 1080, Matilda was intermittently at war with him until his death in 1106, sometimes wearing armour to lead her own troops. In 1082 she sent part of the famous treasure of Canossa to Rome to finance the Pope's military operations.

In 1089, at the age of forty-three, Matilda married the seventeen-year-old Welf V, duke of Bavaria and Carinthia, a member of the Este family. They separated six years later, Henry IV taking the Este side in the resulting quarrel. Matilda encouraged Henry's son, Conrad, to rebel against his father and seize the crown of Italy. She finally made peace with Henry IV's successor, Henry V, willing her private territorial possessions to him, although she had already donated them to the papacy, an act that later provoked controversy between papacy and empire.

Buried near Mantua, she was held in such high regard by succeeding popes that her remains were removed to Rome in 1634 by Pope Urban VIII, and finally re-interred in St. Peter's.

The Knights of Tau

It is our will and command that the hospice and its brethren build and maintain upon the public pilgrim's highway near Ficeclum on the White Arno, at the most convenient point, a bridge for the service of travellers, and this without let or hindrance from any person whomsoever. But if, in case of flood or other accident, they shall be without a bridge, it is our will that they provide a ferry-boat for the free transportation of pilgrims, and it shall be unlawful for any other person to keep any boat there for passengers, whether for hire or not.

The Order of Saint James of Altopascio, also called the Knights of the Tau or Hospitallers of Saint James, was a military order, perhaps the earliest Christian institution to combine the protection and assistance of pilgrims, the staffing of hospitals, with a military role. The name comes from the long black mantle the friars wore, on which was the taumed cross. This decoration was considered, by some, to be a symbol of the cross and the final letter of the Hebrew alphabet. Usually white on a black field, the vertical arm of the tau is always pointed at the bottom and the crossbar either square or else concave or notched like a Maltese cross, the result being called a *croce taumata*. Some historians suggest that the sign represents an auger and an axe or hammer, and thus the carpentry associated with the bridge-building and road maintenance carried out by the knights.

The Order is said, by some, to have been founded by Matilda of Canossa between 1070 and 1080, though according to the Order's own tradition, it was founded between the Palude di Fucecchio, the Lago di Sesto, and the forest of Cerbaie by twelve citizens of nearby Lucca, a tradition which is preserved in a couple of lines of poetry appended to the Italian version of its rule:

La qual casa sia questa dell' Ospitale
La quale incommincio lo Coro duodenale.

That house which belongs to the hospital
Which was founded by the Choir of twelve.

Originally the Order was composed of a few canons charged with caring for pilgrims on their way to Rome or the Holy Land, via Italy, but later it extended its concern to the Way of Saint James. The Order had a bell named *La Smarrita*, which was rung each night to help guide to safety any pilgrim wandering in the woods.

The fortunes of the knights prospered thanks to the support of popes and emperors for their philanthropic activity which, over time, transcended the original goal to maintain the via Romea and protect those following it. In 1244 the hospice of Altopassus received a confirmation of its properties in Italy from the Emperor Frederick II, as part of a program of support for institutions looking after the *miserabiles* (unfortunate). The emperor forbade the imposition of any tax on the Order or any interference, lay or ecclesiastical, with its property.

Like many of their secular and religious counterparts, the Order of St. James of Altopascio began its decline in the 1300s. The knights, who had once been valiant defenders of the pilgrims of Christendom, had given in to sloth and worldliness. There were even some cases of the Order accepting married men.

In 1239, Pope Gregory IX reformed their rule of life to a variation of that of the Knights of St. John – known today as the Knights of Malta – in an attempt to reintroduce a rigorous interior life into the Order.

In 1587, Pope Pius II suppressed the Order by transferring the lands to the Order of Our Lady of Bethlehem. Nevertheless, the Order retained some Italian property until 1587, when Sixtus V, at the request of the Grand Duke of Tuscany, merged the Order of Altopascio with the Order of Saint Stephen.

After Altopascio, the route takes you through woods and an evocative rendezvous with the via Francigena's history. The boundary stone in Pietra Siena, installed during the Grand Duchy of Peter Leopold II, bears the reference No.13, which relates to a report made on the condition of the road in 1812, which was described as being "in an appalling state."

After this, you will cross the Greppi bridge, wooden today and most probably wooden when it was first built, but replaced by brick in the 18th century. The bridge was the principal link road between the Valdarno and the area of Lucca served by the via Francigena. It finally collapsed in the 20th century, but one pillar came to light during recent archaeological excavations.

Situated in a barycentric position up on the Cerbaie hills, the village of Galleno can be identified with the *Grasse Geline* mentioned by Philip Augustus of France, on his return trip from his 3rd crusade. He described it as an intermediate stage .

The word *Cerbaie* probably originates from *cerraie,* which means Turkey Oak forest, due to the abundance of this type of tree. The forest covering these hills today is renowned for the variance of species, plant and animal. At this point of the via Francigena, the route is surrounded by a typical mixed oak wood with Chestnut trees, Durmast oak and Holly. Deeper in the valley one finds a marsh forest of Black Alder, English oak, White Hornbeam or Narrow Leaved Ash, a relic of the ancient preneolithic lowland forest. On the hill summit, there is a mixed forest of Turkey Oak and more Mediterranean species like the Strawberry Tree, heathers, Flowering ash and strips of Maritime Pine forest.

As you walk along the cobbled path, it is sobering to think that you are probably walking on the same stones as your counterparts, centuries before.

Ponte a Cappiano XXIII Aqua Nigra

Leaving Altopascio and beyond Galleno, the road runs downhill towards Padule di Fucecchio, and passes the site where the monastery and parish church of Cappiano once stood. Here, it reaches the bridge of the same name built in the 16th century by Antonio and Francesco of Sangallo, in order to regulate the waters and increase the numbers of fish. The construction is huge and more accurately described as an elongated building suspended over the waters of what used to be the greatest inner marsh in Italy.

Interestingly, in terms of the via Francigena, the Medici bridge was put in place when the area was little more than a system of waterways, which means that though Sigeric listed the *submansione* as number XXIII, it is likely there was no settlement and he travelled past by boat. The bridge was destroyed in 1325 during the war between Lucca and Florence and rebuilt again by the monks of the Badia a Settino.

Given the strategic importance of its position, the bridge was fortified with a tower and three draw bridges in the late 14th century. In the drawing by Leonardo da Vinci, the structure was equipped with a lock, used both for eel fishing and controlling the flow of water from the swamp. In the early 16th century the bridge was rebuilt with its present day structure by order of Cosimo de Medici. Today pilgrims can sleep in the hostel built into the Medici bridge.

Fucecchio XXIII Arne Blanca

The origin and history of Fucecchio are tightly bound to those of the via Francigena, whose route at that particular segment is intersected by the River Arno. Around the 10th century, the Cadolingi, originally from Pistoia, focused on this important junction and built Salamarzana Castle. After the Cadolingi rule, Fucecchio, now a free municipality, began to show signs of development in the 16th century, with the recovery of agricultural activities, from which originate some of the great farms that once belonged to the Medici family.

In the historic centre, the evocative complex of Palazzo Corsini rises in the town's original centre. From the 10th century it was the headquarters of the Salamarzana Castle, and transformed during the 14th century into a fortress by the Florentines. Having lost its military importance, it was acquired by Giovanni di Cosimo dei Medici, the father of Lorenzo the Magnificent, who turned it into a farm. In 1643, the entire complex passed to the Corsini and, in 1981, to the Municipality, making it available to the community by housing the Fucecchio Civic Museum, the historical archive and the library.

Of particular interest:

The historic Abbey of San Salvatore was founded in the 10th century by the Cadolingi family, and is home to a precious Crucifix from the early 1300s, a splendid 17th-century organ and several paintings by Empoli and Caccini.

The Collegiate Church of San Giovanni Battista, houses the beautiful panel painting depicting the Madonna and Child Enthroned with Saints (1526) by Bartolomeo Ghetti.

The historic Palazzo Montanelli Della Volta, also the home of the Montanelli Bassi Foundation, was founded in 1987 by the renowned journalist Indro Montanelli to endorse the cultural and historical heritage of his home town.

San Miniato

After Fucecchio the route crosses the Arno, over a modern bridge at San Pierino, where an archaeological dig recently brought to light some Medieval remains, and a section of pavement relating to the via Francigena.

Archaeological evidence indicates that the site of the city and surrounding area has been settled since at least the Palaeolithic era. It would have been well known to the Etruscans, and certainly to the Romans, for whom it was a military post called Quarto.

The first mention in historical documents is of a small village organised around a chapel dedicated to San Miniato, built by the Lombards in 783. By the end of the 10th century San Miniato boasted a sizeable population, enclosed behind a moat and protected by a castle built by Otto I, from which an Imperial Vicar ruled all of Tuscany. The first walls, with defensive towers, were built in the 12th century, during the time when Italy was dominated by Frederick Barbarossa. Under his grandson, Frederick II, the town was further fortified with expanded walls and other defensive works, including the Rocca and its tower.

Of particular interest:

The Church of San Domenico, with its unfinished façade, stands in Piazza del Popolo. It contains frescoes and paintings by the 14th to 18th century Florentine school.

The Cathedral is a Latin cross church, dedicated to both Sant'Assunta and Santo Genesio. Originally Romanesque but remodelled during the centuries, it also has Gothic and Renaissance elements. Look out for the distinctive coloured majolica bowls on the façade. The cathedral's campanile is known as the Matilde Tower and is known for its asymmetrical clock.

The Museo Diocesano di Arte Sacra (Diocesan Museum of Sacred Art), houses the beautiful 13th century majolica tondoes, which were removed from the façade of the cathedral, and works by Filippo Lippi, Il Empoli, Neri di Bicci, Fra Bartolomeo, Frederico Cardi (known as Cigoli) and Verrocchio.

The Palazzo Vescovile is a 13th century palace that has been renovated several times over the centuries.

The Episcopal Seminary and Piazza del Seminario have a particular shape, influenced by the winding of the ancient walls that were leaning against primitive homes.

The Palazzo Comunale is a 14th century building and is still San Miniato's Town Hall.

Palazzo Grifoni is one of the most conspicuous examples of civil architecture from the Tuscan Renaissance. The palace is home to the Cassa di Risparmio di San Miniato, and was bombed by the Germans in the summer of 1944, then restored and rebuilt in the 1990s.

The Tower at the top of the hill, known as Friederick's tower, was the prison of Pier delle Vigne, one of Friederick II's stewards. He killed himself there, as recounted in Dante's Divine Comedy. During World War II, the tower was destroyed by the German Army to prevent the Allies from using it as a gun-sighting tower, but reconstructed in 1958.

The Santuario del Santissimo Crocifisso di Castelvecchio was commissioned by Bishop Poggi of San Miniato, and built by the citizens to preserve the image of the Miraculous Crucifix of Castelvecchio, a wooden crucifix from the 11th century. According to legend, it was abandoned in San Miniato by two travellers.

In 1211 when he visited the city, Saint Francis of Assisi is said to have founded the Convent of San Francesco. The Convent stands behind the city, higher up on the hill, and has a Romanesque façade. Its interior features Gothic-style chapels and frescoes from the 14th and 15th centuries.

The Monastery of Santa Chiara in San Miniato was founded in 1226, and housed Clarisse nuns for several centuries before it was transformed into a conservatory for educating young girls, following the suppression of religious orders in 1785. Today, the convent's rooms are open to visitors, as well as the church and the chapel dedicated to St. Mary Magdalene. The rich collection on display was collected throughout the centuries, from the dowries of sisters who took their vows in the convents. The church boasts priceless 17th century decorations by the workshop of the painter Antonio Domenico Bamberini. Inside, there are various paintings of considerable quality, including paintings, urns, liturgical objects and embroideries made by the nuns. In addition to a beautiful painting by Cigoli, the furnishings are interesting as well, such as two Medieval crucifixes, the first made by Deodato Orlandi in 1301 and the second attributed to the Sienese Jacopo di Mino del Pellicciaio from around 1340.

Pietro della Vigna

Born in 1190 in Capua, in humble circumstances, Pietro della Vigna studied law in Bologna. Through his classical education, his ability to speak Latin and his poetic gifts, he gained the favour of Emperor Frederick II, who made him his secretary, and afterwards *judex magnae curiae*, councillor, governor of Apulia, prothonotary and chancellor. He proved a skillful and trustworthy diplomat, and persistently defended the emperor against his traducers and against the pope's opposition. However, in spite of his apparently exemplary service, Pietro dell Vigna was arrested in Cremona as a traitor, in 1249. Though the reasons for his arrest have never been clarified, a conspiracy or accusation of corruption has been suggested. Falsely accused of *lèse-majesté*, he was imprisoned, blinded and committed suicide soon after.

In Dante's Divine Comedy, Virgil and Dante come upon a dark forest filled with old, gnarled trees and devoid of any greenery. Harpies roost in the trees and release terrible shrieks. Virgil tells Dante that they are now in the second ring of the seventh circle of hell, and that he should pluck a small branch from a tree. When Dante does this, the tree cries out in pain, asking him "Why dost thou rend my bones?". Virgil apologizes to the tree but says that only by plucking a branch could Dante believe that the trees used to be people. Virgil then asks the tree to tell Dante who it used to be. The tree says that he was the man who held the keys to Frederick II's heart, but that other people convinced Frederick to distrust him and in despair he, the faithful servant, killed himself. Though he does not identify himself by name, he is Pier delle Vigne.

On hearing Pier della Vigna's story, Dante is so moved by pity that he cannot speak. Instead, he asks Virgil to speak for him.

The poet waited briefly, then said
to me: "Since he is silent, do not lose
this chance, but speak and ask what you would know."
And I: "Do you continue; ask of him
whatever you believe I should request;
I cannot, so much pity takes my heart." (Inf. XIII, 79-84)

Pier, the tree, replies and begs Dante to ameliorate his bad reputation back on earth, because his reputation is the only part of him surviving outside hell. He then explains that when someone commits suicide, his or her soul is sent by Minos to the seventh circle of hell, where it falls in the forest, sprouts "like a corn of wheat" and grows into a tree. The harpies then feed on the trees' leaves, which causes great pain.

Leaving San Miniato the route follows small roads and then moves up into the hills of the Elsa Valley, which is dotted with the castles and hospitals that Sigeric would have also encountered.

Of particular interest:

The parish Church of Coiano, with its steep flight of steps.

The church in Chianni, a beautiful example of 12th century late-Romanesque architecture.

Borgo Santo Genesio XXII Sce Dionisii

Colanno XXI Sce Peter Currant

Gambassi Terme XX Sce Maria Glan

The territory around Gambassi Terme was densely populated from the 7th century BC, until the Late-Roman age in the 3rd century AD. Its history is heavily influenced by its position and featured as a transit route for the Etruscans and later the Romans on the via Clodia, which linked Lucca with Rome. The town was also used as a stopping place for pilgrims on the via Francigena, The establishment of a hospice was recorded in the 13th century. Between the 12th and 13th centuries the inhabitants of Gambassi Terme enjoyed relative autonomy and prosperity, but this ended when the town was absorbed into the district of San Gimignano. A harsh conflict took place as a result, with considerable loss of life and property. Eventually, the castle of Gambassi was annexed to the territories under the powerful jurisdiction of Florence. Some centuries later, from the Middle Ages to the modern era, the area around Gambassi became known for its glass production, but since 1977, Gambassi Terme has become primarily known as a spa resort, because the waters are proven to be therapeutic and curative for many ailments.

The parish of St Peter and Paul is documented as a halting place along the via Francigena. A Romanesque construction with a basilica form, it has three naves, which meet together in a single apse. The oldest part of the church is the presbytery zone made from sand stone, while the first bays and the façade in brickwork date back to the end of the 12th century. The upper section of the façade is decorated with rows of small suspended arches that were once topped by ceramic basins.

The Holy Mount of San Vivaldo

Also called the "Jerusalem of Tuscany", San Vivaldo dates back to early 1300, when the Franciscan friar, Vivaldo Stricchi, retired to a hermitic life, but was later found dead in the trunk of a chestnut tree that used to be his home.

Located on a rural hillside, outside the town, the former hermitage site was dramatically developed in 1500, with the arrival of the Franciscan Minor Friars. The friars created the Sacro Monti, otherwise known as the Jerusalem of Tuscany. The design was principally the work of the friar, Tommaso da Firenze, his goal being to enable people who could not go on a pilgrimage to the Holy Land, due to the Ottoman occupation of Palestine, to nevertheless benefit from the symbolic experience. For this, he created the topographical and architectural mirror of 15th century Jerusalem. The eighteen distinct chapels, putatively corresponding to sites of the Holy Land, and containing vivid polychrome statuary groupings recalling events of the New Testament.

The sanctuary of the Pancole

The sanctuary is situated approximately five kilometres before San Gimignano. In the place where the church now stands, there was once a niche, on which Pier Francesco Fiorentino painted the Virgin Mary nursing the baby Jesus. Legend has it that in April of 1668, Bartolomea Ghini, a shepherdess, who was born mute, was feeling particularly despondent about her impoverished state, and was crying as she led her flock to the pasture. Suddenly, a beautiful woman appeared in front of her and

asked why she was so sad. When Bartolomea answered, the woman told her to go home, where she would find a pantry full of bread, and overflowing barrels of wine. Bartolomea suddenly realized that she had actually spoken and ran home, yelling for her parents at the top of her lungs. They were amazed both at hearing their daughter speak and seeing the pantry filled. All of the villagers went to the pasture where the girl claimed to have seen this mysterious woman, but found nothing except a heap of brambles. After stripping everything back, they finally discovered that the thorns had been hiding the niche with an image, which, according to Bartolomea, depicted the same woman she had just met. While the brambles were being removed, the icon was scratched by a pruning hook, and the mark is still visible.

The news drew a multitude of pilgrims, who brought special offerings and materials to build a church to house the image. The building was erected and consecrated within just two years, though in 1944, retreating Germans almost completely destroyed it. Only the altar wall, with the sacred image was saved, but a small chapel was rebuilt and the sanctuary reconsecrated on October 19, 1949. In addition to Pier Francesco Fiorentino's image of the Virgin nursing the baby Jesus, the inside also houses two wooden polychrome sculptures from the 17th century, depicting Saint Julietta with her son Quriaqos and Saint Geminiano, both from the Church of San Quirico.

San Gimignano XIX Sce Gemiane

The foundation of San Gimignano dates back to ancient times. According to legend, in 63 B.C. two brothers, Muzio and Silvio, two young patricians escaping from Rome after their implication in the conspiracy of Catiline, sheltered in Valdelsa and built two castles: the Castle of Mucchio and the Castle of Silvia, which would develop into the future San Gimignano.

The first historical document mentioning the name of the town

is dated 30th August 929, when Ugo di Provenza donated to the Bishop of Volterra the so-called Mount of the Tower *prope Sancto Geminiano adiacente* (next to San Gimignano). The name of San Gimignano probably comes from the bishop of Modena. According to legend, during the barbaric invasions the saint appeared miraculously on the city walls, and saved the town from Totila's threat.

San Gimignano, is famous for its fascinating Medieval architecture and seventy-two towers rising above of all the other buildings, though today only thirteen towers remain. The small town was developed through the establishment of a market selling products brought in from the nearby countryside, and sold to pilgrims and the hospices that had opened for them. San Gimignano also benefited from its position on the road from Pisa, meaning that the Sienese could reach the town while also avoiding the lower Elsa valley and lower Valdarno, both of which were controlled by the Florentines.

In Medieval times the tower was a symbol of power, mainly because the building process was neither simple nor cheap. Materials needed to be dug and transferred to town, and the building site arranged. Only the richest families of merchants and moneylenders could afford them. The house only occupied part of the tower, the ground floor consisting of workshops, the first floor of bedrooms, and the higher level the kitchen. From the end of the 12th century, towers built according to the same model were also attached to other buildings of lower height, and could already be defined as *palazzi*. After the first half of the 13th century, palaces built according to the most up-to-date and fashionable trends of that time, were built instead.

Today, the main road between the city gates of San Matteo and San

Giovanni, which skirts around the massive Romanesque parish church (today a collegiate chapel) is in fact the via Francigena, and at least two of the six hospitals documented in the Middle Ages faced directly onto it. The city flourished until 1348, when it was struck by the Black Death that affected all of Europe, and about half the townsfolk died. The diversion of the pilgrim route led to the town's decline, as well as its preservation. In its heyday the town walls enclosed five monasteries, four hospitals, public baths and a brothel, but today, only one of the towers, Torre Grossa, is open to the public. San Gimignano has retained many fine examples of Romanesque and Gothic architecture. As well as churches and Medieval fortifications. There are notable examples of Romanesque secular and domestic architecture, which can be distinguished from each other by their round and pointed arches, respectively. A particular feature, typical of the region of Siena, is that the arches of openings are depressed, with doorways often having a second low arch set beneath a semi-circular or pointed arch. Both Romanesque and Gothic windows sometimes have a bifurcate form, with two openings divided by a stone mullion under a single arch.

Other interesting facts:

San Gimignano is the birthplace of the poet Folgore da San Gimignano (1270–1332).

A fictionalised version of San Gimignano is featured in E. M. Forster's 1905 novel, Where Angels Fear to Tread.

Tea with Mussolini, a 1999 drama about the plight of English and American expatriate women in Italy during World War II, was partially filmed in San Gimignano. The frescoes that the women save from being destroyed during the German Army's withdrawal are inside the Duomo, the town's main church.

Franco Zeffirelli used San Gimignano as a stand-in for the town of Assisi in his 1972 St. Francis of Assisi biopic, Brother Sun, Sister Moon. Most of the Assisi scenes were filmed here.

In his novel, The Broker, by John Grisham, Joel Backman takes his second of three wives on vacation in Italy to keep her from divorcing him. They rent a 14th century monastery near San Gimignano for a month.

M.C. Escher's 1923 woodcut, San Gimignano, depicts the celebrated towers.

Of particular interest:

The Collegiata, with its plain exterior, hides an interior swathed in frescoes. Lippo Memmi on the right wall (1333–41), Bartolo di Fredi the left (1367), Taddeo di Bartolo the Last Judgement in the nave (1410) and Benozzo Gozzoli, St Sebastian (1464).

The Museo Civico - situated on the first floor of the Palazzo del Popolo, houses works by Pinturicchio, Filippino Lippi, Benozzo Gozzoli and Lippo Memmi.

Piazza della Cisterna is a triangular piazza, ringed with 13th and 14th century towers and centred on a 1237 stone well.

Sant'Agostino is a little church most tourists miss, but its Piero di Pollaiuolo altarpiece (1483) and Benozzo Gozzoli's colourful apse frescoes on the life of St Augustine (1465) are well worth making the effort to find, as is the tomb of San Bartolo (1488) against the west wall.

The Museo della Tortura offers a grisly array of torture instruments. The explanatory placards making grim reading.

The Museo Archaeological, houses a small collection of Etruscan artifacts, including a curious funerary urn topped by a reclining effigy of the deceased, his cup holding a coin to pay for entry into the afterlife.

The Museo d'Arte Sacra, a modest museum of liturgical art stands on a pretty piazza off the Collegiata's left flank. Highlights of the collection are a Madonna and Child by Bartolo di Fredi and 14th century illuminated choir books.

Dante Alighieri (1265-1321)

When a person's name recurs so regularly along a single route, he deserves further examination. Dante is best known for his epic poem *La Divina Commedia*, which has profoundly affected not only the religious imagination, but all subsequent allegorical creation of imaginary worlds in literature.

Born into a Florentine family of noble ancestry. Dante received a thorough education in both classical and Christian literature. At the age of twelve, he was promised to his future wife, Gemma Donati, though he had already fallen in love with another girl called Beatrice. She was nine-years-old. The nature of his love had its roots in the Medieval concept of courtly love and the idealization of women.

His mother, Bella degli Abati, died when he was seven-years-old. His father, Alighiero II, who made his living from money-lending and property, remarried, but died himself in the early 1280s, before the future poet reached manhood. Brunetto Latini, a man of letters and a politician, became a father figure for Dante, but later in his Commedia, Dante placed him in hell, among those who were guilty of 'violence against nature' - sodomy.

Dante spent much of his life travelling from one city to another, but this probably had more to do with the restless times, than his wandering character, or fixation on the Odyssey. In 1289, Dante entered politics and joined the Bianchi Guelphs, one of the rival factions within the Guelph party. In 1295 he entered the Guild of Apothecaries, to which philosophers could belong and which gave him entry to public office.

Dante served the commune in various councils and was ambassador to San Gimignano in 1300 and then to Rome. In June 1400, he was appointed superintendent of roads and road repair.

Latterly though, Dante was exiled when the Neri Guelphs, who had the pope's support, ascended to power. The Bianchi Guelphs were condemned to death by burning should they ever be caught again in Florence, but they soon made an alliance with the Ghibelline party and attempted several unsuccessful attacks on Florence. Their hopes ended with the death (1313) of the emperor Henry VII. Dante was charged with financial corruption in January 1302 and some months later he was condemned to death by burning.

After 1302, Dante never saw his home town again, but found shelter in various Italian cities and with such rulers as Ordelaffi of Forli, the Scaligeri of Verona and the Malaspina of Lunigiana. He lived his remaining years in the courts of northern Italian princes. During his exile, and under the patronage of the Ghibelline leaders, he started to write his Commedia, a long story-poem through the three worlds of the afterlife. In 1320 Dante made his final home in Ravenna, where he died on the night of September 13, 1321. His body was brought to the Church of San Francisco. Shortly after he died, Dante was accused of Averroism (the term applied to a philosophical trend among scholastics in the late 13th century) and his book, De Monarchia, was burned by the order of Pope John XXII.

When enough time had passed to heal old wounds, in this case two hundred years, his work proved to be a beloved masterpiece and Florence decided they wanted their poet back, even building a beautiful memorial for his remains. In 1519 Pope Leo X ordered the bones to be transferred to Florence, but the papal order was refused. Instead, an empty coffin was sent back, because the Franciscan monks in charge of Dante's remains had secretly removed them from the tomb, and hidden them in their monastery. It's not clear exactly when, but at some point the remains were moved again and ended up in the wall of the church near the tomb. It wasn't until 1865 that the hidden bones were found during some renovations. The mausoleum in Ravenna is a simple marble structure with the poet's tomb inside.

Colle di Val d'Elsa

The name Colle, meaning hillside, stems from its lofty position on a hill in the valley of the river Elsa. Due to its position - close to both Florence and Siena - Colle Val d'Elsa has always been the object of ancient rivalry. The town of Colle was established in Medieval times close to the via Francigena and was one of the protagonists in the fights between Guelphs and Ghibellines. In its heyday, the town was populated by pilgrims and wayfarers, who stopped there to rest at the foot of its characteristic tower houses.

Many Medieval and renaissance buildings of great historical and architectural value are still present in the upper part of the town, and bear witness to this period. The village is entered through the ancient and monumental Porta Nova, and the road winds its long and narrow way to the magnificent Palazzo Campana, which marks the entry to the Castle. Here, the atmosphere suddenly changes and one follows narrow paved lanes, between magnificent 15th and 16th century noble houses, one of them being where sculptor and architect Arnolfo di Cambio was born.

Another interesting feature is that Colle Val d'Elsa has been the capital of crystal for centuries, so much so that it's been nicknamed the Bohemia of Italy. Chalices, plates and glasses are created with a mix of mastery and technique still observed today, making the town the producer of nearly all the crystal manufactured in Italy.

Of particular interest:

The San Pietro Museum, which after almost twenty years of closure, has reopened its doors to the public. Housed in the monumental complex of the Conservatory, visitors will find the Bilenchi Collection and Walter Fusi Collection.

The ex-hospital of San Lorenzo and the ex-conservatory of San Pietro stand in front of one another with the annexed church alongside. Both were built by the powerful Usimbardi family, from which the first bishop of Colle Val d'Elsa was also descended. The ex-conservatory of San Pietro, completed in 1606, was designed by Giorgio Vasari the Younger, and is now a museum. This exhibition complex offers temporary show space, plus the Civic and Diocese Sacred Art Museum, with works ranging from the Medieval era to the 20th century.

As the route takes you back out into the countryside and the most evocative atmosphere of small farm tracks and woodland, look out for the ancient hot spring, where dusty and weary pilgrims may have stopped to take advantage of the natural bounty.

Molino *XVIII Sce Martin in Fosse*

Abbadia a Isola *XVI Burgenove*

Abbadia a Isola is a small, Medieval village, built around the Cistercian Abbey of San Salvatore e Cirino, which was founded there in the 10th century, by Countess Ava di Staggia, as a stopping place for pilgrims along the via Francigena. The name originates from its position in the middle of a huge marshy basin. In the 12th century the Abbey came under the protection of the city of Siena, which fortified it with defensive works and a moat. The complex still retains its Medieval charm with the 11th century church in the Lombard style, best known for the early 16th century fresco by Vincenzo Tamagni, and a 15th century marble baptismal font. The interior of the church has three naves, but only the remains of the bell tower are visible to the right of the sacristy. On the facade of the current church the remains of a twin portal, typical of the pilgrimage churches, can still be seen.

Monteriggioni

Sitting on a small natural hillock, this completely walled Medieval town was built in the 13th century by the overlords of Siena to command the Cassia Road, running through the Val d'Elsa and Val Staggia just to the west of Monteriggioni.

Today, its fortified walls and fourteen heavily fortified towers remain intact and create an unforgettable impression. Two gates lead inside - Porta Franca (or Romea) and Porta di san Romea) and Porta di san Giovanni - and from here one can proceed into the large piazza, with its Romanesque church (13th century), dedicated to the Assumption of the Virgin. It must also be mentioned that Dante used Monteriggioni as a simile for the deepest abyss at the heart of his 'Inferno',

As with circling round
Of turrets, Monteriggioni crowns his walls;
E'en thus the shore, encompassing the abyss,
Was turreted with giants, half their length
Uprearing, horrible, whom Jove from heaven
Yet threatens, when his muttering thunder rolls.

The current structure of the village is essentially the original one, the only changes it went through date back to the 16th century, when the towers were lowered and some earth accumulated at the base of the walls. The second change dates back to 1921 when three of the fourteen towers were reduced to the level of the walls. If you are there in July, you may be able to enjoy the Medieval Festival of Monteriggioni, when the streets are filled with craftsmen, cavaliers and people in period costume.

The castle of La Chiocciola dominates the horizon as you follow the route to Siena. Built in 1555, it takes its name from the beautiful winding stairs which connect the storeys in the cylindrical tower.

Also look out for the oldest tree on the Montagnola, a prime specimen of the Monumental Downy Oak, perfectly adapted to the region because it is drought-resistant and thrives on clay and limestone soils.

Siena XV Seocine

Siena was founded by Senius, son of Remus, who was in turn the brother of Romulus, after whom Rome was named. Statues and other artwork depicting a she-wolf suckling the young twins Romulus and Remus can be seen all over the city of Siena.

A proud, wealthy and warlike independent city-state during the Middle Ages, Siena held off its rival Florence in several battles before finally being defeated. The Historic Centre of Siena is the embodiment of a Medieval city. Throughout the centuries, the city has preserved its Gothic appearance of the 12th and 15th centuries. During this period, the work of Duccio, the Lorenzetti brothers and Simone Martini influenced the course of Italian and, more broadly, European art. The whole city was devised as a work of art blending into the surrounding landscape, spread across three hills and connected by three major streets forming a Y-shape. The seven-kilometre long fortified wall still surrounds the centre. To the west, the walls embrace the Fort of Santa Barbara rebuilt by the Medici in 1560, and finished in 1580. Inside the walls, tower-houses,

palaces, churches and other religious structures survive unchanged. This can be explained in part by the fact that the city did not suffer serious war damage and has been spared from modern industrial development. The city's fountains continue to be fed by an extensive system of original tunnels.

Siena is a perfect place to stay, where the best of Tuscan food and wine seems to be on every corner. If you are feeling in need of a cultural, historical and culinary experience, then take a day out here. There is so much to see and do, but **of particular interest:**

Piazza del Campo, now regarded as one of the most beautiful civic spaces in Europe, occupies the site of the old Roman forum and for much of Siena's early history was the city's principal market place. It began to assume its present shape in 1293, when the Council of Nine, Siena's ruling body at the time, began to acquire land with a view to creating a grand civic piazza. The red-brick paving was begun in 1327 and completed in 1349. The distinctive nine segments were designed to reflect the authority of the Council, and symbolise the protective folds of the Madonna's cloak. The piazza has been the focus of civic life ever since - a setting for executions, bullfights and the twice yearly drama of the Palio.

Fonte Gaia, is a 19th century copy of an original carved by Jacop della Quercia in 1409. The relief depicts the Virtues, Adam and Eve and the Madonna and Child. The water still comes from a 500-year-old aqueduct.

Palazzo Pubblico, Siena's town hall. The Palazzo Pubblico's Medieval rooms, some decorated with paintings from the Sienese School, are open to the public. The main council chamber, or *Sala del Mappamundo*, is

named after a map of the world painted by Ambrogio Lorenzetti in the early 14th century. One wall is covered in Simone Martini's recently restored fresco of the Maesta (1315), which depicts the Virgin in Majesty as the Queen of Heaven, attended by the Apostles, saints and angels. Opposite is a fresco of the mercenary Guidoriccio da Fogliano (1330). The walls of the chapel alongside, are covered with frescoes of the 'Life of the Virgin' (1407) by Taddeo di Bartolo, and the choir stalls are decorated with wooden panels inlaid with biblical scenes.

The Sala della Pace contains the famous 'Allegory of Good and Bad Government' (1338-40), a pair of frescoes by Ambrogio Lorernzetti . They form one of the most important series of secular paintings from the Middle Ages. In the Good Government fresco, civic life flourishes, while the Bad Government is presided over by a demon, and shows rubbish-strewn streets and ruins.

The Sala del Risorimento is covered with late 19th century frescoes illustrating the events leading up to the unification of Italy under King Vittorio Emanuele II. The entrance to the Torre del Mangia, the palace's bell tower is in the palace courtyard. Rising one hundred and two metres high, the tower was built by the brothers Muccio and Francesco di Rinaldo between 1338 and 1348, and named after the first bell ringer, whose idleness led to the nickname *Mangiaguadagni* (eat the profits). There are five hundred and five steps to the top of the tower, but the incredible view makes the strain worthwhile.

Santuario e Casa di Santa Caterina is named after Siena's patron saint Catherine Beneincasa (1347-80). At the age of eight she devoted herself to God and had many visions, as well as later receiving the stigmata. Like her namesake, St Catherine of Alexandria, she was believed to have been betrothed to the Christ Child in a vision - a scene that inspired many artists. Her eloquence persuaded Pope Gregory XI to return the seat of the papacy to Rome in 1376. After sixty-seven years of exile in Avignon. St Catherine died in Rome and was canonized in 1461. Today, Catherine's house is surrounded by chapels and cloisters. The house itself is decorated with paintings and events from her life by a number of artists, including Francesco Vanni and Pietro Sorn.

Siena's Duomo is one of Italy's greatest cathedrals. Among its treasures, one can see sculptural works by Nicola Pisano, Donatello and Michelangelo. You are advised to take time out to see the pulpit panels, carved in 1265 by Nicola Pisano, and the Massacre of the Innocents (an inlaid marble floor), the Piccolomini Library, famous for its frescoes depicting the life of the Piccolomini Pope, Pius II.

Palazzo Piccolomini is Siena's most imposing private palazzo and built for the wealthy Piccolomini family in the 1460's, by the Florentine architect and sculptor Bernado Rossalini. It now contains the Sienese state archives, account books and taxation documents dating back to the 13th century. Some of the leading artists of their day were employed to paint the wooden bindings used to enclose the tax and account records. The paintings, now on display in the Sala di Congresso, often show scenes of Siena itself, and episodes from the city's past.

Pinacotela Nazionale is a gallery housed in the 14th century Palazzo Buonsignori, and contains a collection of paintings by artists of the Sienese school, including: Duccio's Madonna dei Francescani and Simone Martini's The Blessed Agostino Novello and Four of his Miracles.

The Museo dell'Opera del Duomo is partially is devoted to items removed from the Duomo, including a *rondo* of a Madonna and Child, probably by Donatello. The highlight is Duccio's Maestà (1308-11), one of the Sienese School's finest works.

Fortezza Medicea , a huge red-brick fortress, built for Cosimo I, by Baldassarre Lanci in 1560, following Siena's defeat by the Florentines in the

1554 war. The fortress now houses the Enoteca Italica, a wine shop offering visitors the chance to taste and buy a comprehensive list of wines from all over Italy.

The Hospital Santa Maria della Scala partially gets its name from its position. Located across from Siena Cathedral in Piazza del Duomo, Santa Maria della Scala refers to its position across from the steps leading into the Cathedral. The Hospital is made up of a complex of buildings, which have been enlarged and improved over the years.

From the earliest documentation, the hospital was used as a shelter for foreigners, for the most part pilgrims and travellers following the Francigena. Later, it specialized in supporting and caring for abandoned children in the so-called *Casa delle Balie.* Meticulous records were kept of the details relating to each child. At age eight, they were taught a trade and any profits they made were kept for them. When they reached eighteen, the children had the option of leaving with all their saved earnings, plus one hundred *soldi*, a set of clothing, and furnishings for a house. Girls were given an additional fifty as a dowry. In addition, meals were served to the poor three times a week and the sick were given free treatment.

The Hospital's treatment of the sick was unusual for the time. Their policy was to have one bed for each sick patient, and the sheets were kept clean. Also, in what has been suggested as "one of the earliest examples of such a therapeutic objective," patients were treated in order to be cured. The Hospital employed one doctor and one surgeon. In the 16th century, it added an additional surgeon. As the Hospital became a training ground for doctors, there was, for the 17th and 18th centuries, a unique emphasis on using a more hands-on learning approach. Pilgrims were also included in their programme, receiving free room and board in the pilgrimage halls, and when they left, vouchers for food and drink in the Sienese territory, as they continued their travels.

In 1995, the Hospital opened up to the public as a museum, though it continues to offer accommodation to via Francigena pilgrims. There are nearly 12,000 square meters of paths covering the renovated parts of the Hospital. Of particular interest are the Pellegrinaio, Cappella del Manto, Sagrestia Vecchia, Cappella della Madonna and the Oratories of the Compagnia di Santa Caterina della Notte and of Santa Maria sotto le colte. The ravaged sculptures by Jacopo della Quercia from the Fonte Gaia are displayed here, as well as drawings and models for the 1858 restoration.

Il Palio

This is a horse race held twice a year, in which ten horses and riders, riding bareback and dressed in the appropriate colours, represent ten of the seventeen *Contrade*, or city wards. Each is named after an animal or symbol, and each has a long history and complicated heraldic and semi-mythological associations. The Palio, held on July 2, is known as the *Palio*

di Provenzano, in honour of Madonna di Provenzano, whose church is in Siena. The Palio held on August 16, is named *Palio dell'Assunta,* in honour of the Assumption of Mary.

A magnificent pageant, the *Corteo Storico*, precedes the race, which attracts visitors and spectators from all around the world. The race itself, involves circling the Piazza del Campo three times and usually lasts no more than seventy seconds. It is not uncommon for jockeys to be thrown off their horses, and not unusual to see unmounted horses finishing the race. The Palio is in fact won by the horse representing its *contrada* and not by the jockeys. The earliest known antecedents of the race are Medieval. The town's central piazza was the site of a range of largely combative public games, but the public races organised by the Contrade only became popular from the 14th century on. Called *Palii alla lunga*, they were run across the whole city. When the Grand Duke of Tuscany outlawed bullfighting in 1590, the Contrade took to organising races in the Piazza del Campo. The first such races were on buffalo and called *bufalate*. The donkey-back races later took their place, while horse-racing continued elsewhere. The first modern Palio, called *palio alla tonda* to distinguish it from the earlier *pali alla lunga* took place in 1656. At first, one race was held each year, on July 2. A second, on August 16, was added later.

Tartuca (Tortoise)

Iconic riders

Bastiancino was born in 1745 and was just fourteen when he first raced and won for the Goose contrade. In all he won fifteen times for nine contradas. His extraordinary career ended in 1780, when he fell from his horse and died. He was just thirty-five.

Gobbo Saragiolo was born in 1809 and also made his debut at just fourteen years of age for Chiocciola in 1823, and ended up winning. Throughout his career he was very well known for his ability to win even when he didn't have a good horse. Contradas would pay him huge sums of money to have him ride their horses. All he cared about was money, in fact he represented two enemy contradas: Torre and Oca.

Horses are frequently badly injured and have to be put down by vets, with animal rights campaigners regularly calling for the event to be banned.

Saint Catherine of Siena

Caterina di Giacomo di Benincasa was born on 25 March 1347 in Siena. As a child she was so merry that the family gave her the pet name of *Euphrosyne*, which is Greek for joy. Catherine is said to have had her first vision of Christ when she was five. When she was sixteen, her sister

Bonaventura died and her parents told her that she had to marry Bonaventura's widower. Catherine was absolutely opposed and started to fast as a protest. She would later advise Raymond of Capua to do during times of trouble what she did as a teenager: "Build a cell inside your mind, from which you can never flee." Catherine resisted the accepted course of marriage and motherhood on the one hand, and a nun's veil on the other. Instead, she chose to live an active and prayerful life outside a convent's walls following the model of the Dominicans. Later, her vision of Saint Dominic made her want to join his Order, but in the meantime she became seriously ill, which conveniently helped her mother to persuade her truculent daughter to join the Mantellate - the local association of Dominican tertiaries. Within days of joining the Sisters, Catherine got out of bed and donned the black and white habit of the Third Order of Saint Dominic. But in addition, she received the habit of a Dominican tertiary from the friars of the order, after vigorous protests from the tertiaries themselves, who up to that point had been only widows. As a tertiary, she lived outside the convent, at home with her family just as before, though she lived in almost total silence and solitude.

At the age of twenty-one, Catherine experienced what she described in her letters as a "Mystical Marriage" with Jesus, during which he told her to give up her withdrawn life and enter the public forum. From here, her pious activities in Siena attracted a group of followers, women and men, who gathered around her.

As social and political tensions mounted in Siena, Catherine found herself drawn to the politics of the time and began travelling with her followers throughout northern and central Italy, advocating reform of the clergy and advising people that repentance and renewal could be done through "the total love for God". She also began dictating letters to scribes, thus widening her audience to include figures in authority, as she begged for peace between the republics and principalities of Italy and for the return of the Papacy from Avignon to Rome.

Catherine returned to Siena and spent the early months of 1377 founding a women's monastery of strict observance, outside the city in the old fortress of Belcaro. She spent the rest of 1377 at Rocca d'Orcia, about twenty miles from Siena, on a local mission of peace-making and preaching. During this period, she wrote the Dialogue, in which she described Christ as being the bridge between the soul and God, basing much of her argument on her own mystical experience.

For many years she had accustomed herself to rigorous abstinence, which appeared unhealthy in the eyes of the clergy and her own sisterhood. Her confessor, Raymond of Capua, ordered her to eat properly, but Catherine claimed that she was unable to, describing her inability to eat as an *infermità* (illness). From the beginning of 1380, Catherine could neither eat, nor swallow water. She died in Rome, on 29 April 1380, at the age of thirty-three.

Isola d'Arbia

This little village is home to the Romanesque church of Sant'Ilaro, (Hilary of Poitiers) the French saint, whose worship was widespread in Italy thanks to the via Francigena. The only ornamentation is a frieze of arches made of serpentine marble.

Hilary of Poitiers

Sometimes referred to as the *Hammer of the Arians,* Hilary was the Bishop of Poitiers. His name comes from the Latin word for happy or cheerful. Hilary was born in Poitiers, either at the end of the 3rd or beginning of the 4th century A.D. He spent nearly four years in exile, although the reasons for his banishment remain obscure. The traditional explanation is that Hilary was exiled for refusing to subscribe to the condemnation of the Athanasius and Nicene faiths. More recently several scholars have suggested that political opposition to Constantius and support of the usurper Silvanus may have been the real cause. Nevertheless, while in Phrygia, he continued to govern his diocese, as well as writing two of the most important of his contributions to dogmatic and polemical theology: the *De synodis or De fide Orientalium.*

Hilary spent two or three years trying to persuade the local clergy that the *homoion* confession was merely a cover for traditional Arian subordination. In 364, he extended his efforts once more beyond Gaul, impeaching Auxentius, bishop of Milan as heterodox. Upon returning home, Hilary published the *Contra Arianos vel Auxentium Mediolanensem liber,* in which he described his unsuccessful efforts against Auxentius. Hilary is the pre-eminent Latin writer of the 4th century. Augustine of Hippo called him "the illustrious doctor of the churches", and his works continued to be highly influential in later centuries.

Cuna

The route takes you past Cuna Grange, an excellently conserved example of a fortified Medieval farm and unusual for its size. There are also traces of a *spedale* established there in the 12th century by the Hospice of Santa Maria della Scala of Siena, to give assistance to pilgrims travelling on the via Francigena.

Ponte d'Arbia XIV Arbia

This, otherwise unremarkable town, is nevertheless notable for its exceptional bridge, from which it derives its name, with the 6th century stage post and portico at one extreme, and mill at the other.

Buonconvento

Buonconvento, from the Latin b*onus conventus*, means happy place. Though a small town, the local museum of art houses works by Duccio di Buoninsegna, Pietro Lorenzetti, Andrea di Bartolo, Matteo di Giovanni and other Tuscan painters.

The name Osenna was in use until the 17th century and probably referred to a watercourse, which has now disappeared. The place-name is Etruscan and perhaps *Orcia*, meaning water, stream or brook, is pre-Roman. From the beginning of the 11th century, the name of San Quirico in Osenna is mentioned more frequently, especially in connection with travel along the via Francigena. If you have time in the next section, take a detour to Abbadia San Salvatore, one of the oldest monasteries in Tuscany, and in the Middle Ages an important station on the via Francigena. In 1035, at the peak of its temporal and spiritual powers, the abbey was rebuilt and reconsecrated by Abbot Winizzo, and eventually incorporated into the Medici state in 1559.

Today, the main street, via Dante Alighieri, is the heart of the town. At one end stands the Collegiata and at the other the Church of Santa Maria Assunta, with its fantastical Medieval bestiary adorning the portal. Further along via Dante Alighieri there is the main square and entrance to the Renaissance gardens, *Horti Leonini.*

Of particular interest:

The Collegiate Church of San Quirico. Once a rural church, was rebuilt into the current structure in the 12th century. The rear section was altered in 1663 to add the choir. It is built on the Latin cross plan, with a single nave and side chapels. Notable is the main portal, in Lombard style, with columns supported by lions. The arch includes ten columns, whose capitals are decorated with animals and vegetable figures, while the architrave features, bizarrely, two crocodiles facing each other. The lunette has a high-relief sculpture, allegedly portraying St. Damasus, though likely to be identified with St. Quiricus. A side portal, added in the 13th century, has been attributed to Giovanni Pisano, who was in Siena at the time. Most of the interior decorations date to the 17th century, while the bell tower was rebuilt in 1798.

Santa Maria Assunta, dating from the 12th century, has a plain rectangular plan with a wall covering in square stone. Outside, the massive portal is embellished with decorations that may originate from the Abbazi di Sant'Antimo. The gabled bell tower and the vestry are original too. The apse is crowned with corbels and decorated with suspended arches. On the left side there is another monumental portal whose arch is supported by two columns and contains a decorated shape. The extremely plain interior is lit up by narrow slits, one in the apse.

You are now traversing through what could be described as Tuscany at its best. Hills and valleys, some covered in woodlands, others vineyards, interspersed with churches and tiny villages, such as Vignoni Alto.

Vignoni Alto is simply charming. A tiny, peaceful village on top of a summit that offers breathtaking views on every side. Reached after a relatively steep climb, pausing here is entirely excusable and advised for flagging spirits and feet. The Church of San Biagio a Vignoni is of Romanesque origin. Restored inside, it has a single nave and preserves the remains of 14th and 15th century frescoes. The baptismal font, dated 1585, is currently in the collegiate church of San Quirico, and the bronze Crucifix by Giambologna exhibited in the Montalcino museum, also came from this church.

On your way out of the village you will pass what remains of Vignoni castle. During the 11th century it belonged to the Abbazia di S. Antimo and then later ceded to the aristocratic Tignosi family of Rocca d'Orcia. And finally, throughout the 13th and 14th centuries, Vignoni castle along with nearby Bagno Vignoni managed to escape the control of Siena by changing hands to the Salimbeni family. In the present day village, the tower is still visible, though broken off at a sharp angle and topped by a cordon with tiny windows high-up on each side.

Bagno Vignoni

These thermal waters were found, and have been used, since Roman times. At the heart of the village there is a 16th century, rectangular stone tank known as the Square of Sources, and containing the water that comes directly from a subterranean aquifer of volcanic origins. Since the Etruscans and Romans, Bagno Vignoni has been used by eminent personalities such as Pope Pius II, Saint Catherine of Siena, Lorenzo the Magnificent and many other artists. Bagno Vignoni is still an exclusive retreat, and outside the average pilgrim budget, but simply sitting alongside to appreciate what is an almost eerie phenomenon of nature, is restorative in itself.

San Pellegrino alle Briccole

Mentioned as *Abricula* by Sigeric during his journey in the last decade of the 10th century, the hospice of the Briccole was a major resting place for via Francigena pilgrims. Among its guests were Matilda of Canossa, Philippe Auguste, king of France and Charles d'Anjou's troops. The church still preserves traces of the Romanesque period, such as the masonry work at the base, and the portal with an architrave surmounted by a rounded arch.

Radicofani

For centuries, the imposing Fortress of Radicofani, on the border between Tuscany and Lazio, has been the symbol of defense and control over the via Francigena. This powerful fortification, built on top of a high summit, was built over a long period of time, starting from 978 onwards, though its origins go even further back in time. The thick bastions were capable of resisting the most violent attack, even to artillery fire, while the mighty tower, thirty-seven metres high and rebuilt in the last century, offers enchanting, endless views all over the Val d'Orcia park and the volcanic Monte Amiata.

The most famous personality of Radicofani is Messer Ghino di Tacco, the Gentleman Bandit, or the Italian version of Robin Hood, who lived here at the end of the 13th century, and is also mentioned by both Boccaccio and Dante.

Of particular interest:

The Church of San Pietro Apostolo, with its beautiful Romanesque architecture, is the most important religious place in Radicofani. The interiors are wonderfully decorated with oil paintings, frescoes and a collection of terracotta pieces from the Della Robbia workshop, as well as wooden sculptures.

The Church of Sant'Agata is opposite the church of San Pietro in the same little square. Once a convent, it has been beautifully decorated inside and also houses a precious Madonna with Saints by Andrea Della Robbia.

Radicofani Pass was known as a dangerous place because brigands took advantage of its remoteness to assault pilgrims on their route to Rome. In January 1845 Charles Dickens travelled to Rome along the via Cassia and gave an account of his arrival in Acquapendente.

It was a bad morning when we left Monte Pulciano; and we went, for twelve miles, over a country as barren, as stony, and as wild, as Cornwall in England, until we came to Radicofani, where there is a ghostly, goblin inn: once a hunting-seat, belonging to the Dukes of Tuscany. It is full of such rambling corridors, and gaunt rooms, that all the murdering and phantom tales that ever were written might have originated in that one house. (..) When we got to the mountain pass, which lies beyond this place, the wind (as they had forewarned us at the inn) was so terrific, that we were obliged to take my other half out of the carriage, lest she should be blown over, carriage and all, and to hang to it, on the windy side (as well as we could for laughing), to prevent its going, Heaven knows where. For mere force of wind, this land-storm might have competed with an Atlantic gale, and had a reasonable chance of coming off victorious. (..) There was snow, and hail, and rain, and lightning, and thunder; and there were rolling mists, travelling with incredible velocity. It was dark, awful, and solitary to the last degree; there were mountains above mountains, veiled in angry clouds; and there was such a wrathful, rapid, violent, tumultuous hurry, everywhere, as rendered the scene unspeakably exciting and grand. It was a relief to get out of it, notwithstanding; and to cross even the dismal dirty Papal Frontier (after which we arrived at Acquapendente).

Ghinotto di Tacco

Ghino, was an outlaw and a popular hero in 13th century Italy. Along with his father and brother, he made a career of robbery and plunder, while being hunted down by the Siennese Republic. After they were caught, his father was executed in Siena's Piazza del Campo, while Ghino managed to escape and sought refuge in Radicofani. There, Ghino continued his career as a bandit, but in the manner of a gentleman, always leaving his victims with something to live on. In the Decameron, Boccaccio depicts him as a *Brigante buono*, good brigand, when telling the story of how he kidnapped the Abbot of Cluny. However, Dante, in Canto VI, lines 13–14, of his Purgatorio, points to Ghino's ferocity when he refers to the death of the Aretine Benincasa da Latrina.

Ghino di Tacco piglia l'abate di Clignì e medicalo del male dello stomaco e poi il lascia quale, tornato in corte di Roma, lui riconcilia con Bonifazio papa e fallo friere dello Spedale.	*Ghino di Tacco seizes the Abbot of Cluny, cures him of his stomach ailment and then releases him; the abbot, having returned to the Roman court, reconciles Ghino with Pope Boniface and makes him prior of the Hospital.* Boccaccio

Quiv'era l'Aretin che da le braccia fiere di Ghin di Tacco ebbe la morte.	*Here was the Aretine who met his death at the fierce hands of Ghin di Tacco.* Dante

Voltole X Sce Petirin Pail

Acquapendente IX Aquapendente

First settled by Etruscans, then Romans, Acquapendente was sacked and taken by the Longobards. In the Middle Ages it was established as a village and monastery by the Benedictine order, because of its position on the via Francigena. The town became known as the *Jerusalem of Europe* because of its cathedral dedicated to the Holy Sepulchre. The name of the city, meaning *pending water*, stems from the presence of several small waterfalls forming the Paglia, a stream setting the boundary between Lazio and Tuscany.

Acquapendente also maintains a long tradition called the Pugnaloni. The festival goes back to the 1100s, when the townspeople rebelled against the tyranny of Frederick I Barbarossa (otherwise known as Red Beard). Two farmers came across a miraculously flowering dead cherry tree and took it as a sign from the Madonna del Fiore, the town's protector saint, that they should rise up and seek liberty from tyranny and being successful started a procession to give thanks. Now, on the third Sunday of May, great

masterpieces using flower petals and leaves, are displayed all over town as a symbolic recognition of Madonna of the Flowers and nature itself. The beautiful artworks follow a theme of liberty, nature and religious freedom. The festival also includes a parade, flag throwers and a religious procession.

Of particular interest:

The Cathedral of San Sepolcro is the most significant monument in Acquapendente. Constructed around the year 1000, and with the same dimensions as Christ's sepulchre, over the votive chapel ordered by Matilda of Westphalia. It was consecrated in 1149. After this it was reconstructed several times, and given the title of cathedral in 1649. Following damage during World War II, much of the cathedral was rebuilt, based on the plans developed by Vincenzo Fasolo. Inside, look out for the noteworthy altarpiece in the right transept, a work in enamelled terracotta by Jacopo Beneventano (1522) portraying the Eternal Father worshipped by angels.

The Chapel of St. Hermes venerates the memory of the patron saint, and is particularly interesting for its beautiful 14th century baptismal font under the presbytery, between the two entry stairs. The 10th century crypt was built over the original aedicule (a small shrine) of the Holy Sepulchre set in the middle, and covered by a pyramid with a rectangular base. According to tradition, it holds a stone relic that was bathed in the blood of Christ.

The Tower of Julia di Jacopo is located near the church, and marks the remains of the fortress built by Arrigo IV (currently used as a cultural and welcome centre).

The clock tower (also known as Barbarossa's tower) in the uppermost part of town was part of the imperial castle held by the Swabians for many years.

From Acquapendente, the route offers beautiful and broad views along the slopes of Monti Volsini, with the crater's edge that gradually slopes down into Lake Bolsena. The experience of walking along tracks and dirt roads between vineyards and olive groves is a very real pleasure.

After the end of the Middle Ages, notes left by Medieval travellers and pilgrims become more detailed and include even minor localities, which were not used as stop-overs. The experience of pilgrims was equated to the fight against the 'infidels', since pilgrims considered themselves to be Soldiers of Christ, ready to die for their faith, just as the heroes and martyrs of Roncesvalles.

As you enter the region of Lazio and the outskirts of Bolsena you will see signs pointing to the Brigand's Path, a 100 kilometre ring route, divided into seven stages and following the footsteps of the Cartore Brigands.

The Brigands' Path

Following the via Francigena encompasses themes religious, cultural, historical, culinary and ecological. A smörgåsbord of information and sensations, which should include the phenomenon of Brigandage in southern Italy. An important chapter in the country's post-unification history, and an historic moment that survives more than a century and a half later thanks to the Brigands' Path.

In the beginning the brigands were villagers and mountain men who knew the territory well and, being loyal to the old regime of the House of Bourbon, found themselves forced to change their lives because of the new political system created by the Unification. In short, the popular revolts turned into real rebellions and those who did not want to submit to the oppressors of the era became outlaws. A version of partisanship was formed, fighting in the shadows against the invasion of the House of Savoy, which had increased taxes tenfold for people who were already suffering from hunger, and imposed the military draft on young men whose families needed them to work the land. As a consequence, the brigands opted to live outside the law, often engaging in real banditry including kidnappings for ransom, robbery, violence and other abuses.

Today, the Brigands Path goes through the picturesque village of Cartore, which was the base of the most fearful band of brigands of the time, and gave its name to the collective movement of Cartoran Brigandry.

Fortunato Ansuini

During the 19th century the area across Latium, Umbria and Tuscany, marked the southern border of the Grand Duchy of Tuscany and, since 1861, the Kingdom of Italy and the States of the Church. The area included woodlands such as Selva del Lamone and Monti di Castro, with isolated caves and small rivers. Several brigands used to live here. Fortunato Ansuini was one of these, and known for being extremely cruel. Born in Norcia in 1844 to a family of farmers, Ansuini was forced by his parents to work as a stonemason.

Later, he killed a man in a tavern and was sentenced to eleven years in

prison in Rome, but in May, 1866, he escaped through a drain with three jail mates. The fugitives left Rome and chose Maremma as a secure place to hide. Here, their new life began, involving robberies and racketeering, though the authorities forced them to continuously move from one place to another. Eventually, they were caught while banqueting inside a cave. Ansuini was locked up in the fort Filippo II, but he managed to escape again, with other captives. After breaking their chains, they went out through the window with the help of bed sheets. The next night the brigands stormed a shepherd's house near Capalbio, tied up the family and stole their food, money and guns. Anecdotes about Ansuini are numerous. He liked to mock the authorities, leaving signed letters in the restaurants where he used to eat. Once he went elegantly dressed to Bassano in Teverina and entered the barracks of the carabinieri in the name of a tradesman travelling from Milan. On his request, he received an escort of two gendarmes for personal protection during his journey. At the end, he asked the two men to deliver a letter to their commander explaining how he had been duped.

San Lorenzo Nuovo

The town is located on the northern side of Lake Bolsena's crater rim, and dominates the lake basin on one side and the valley of the Acquapendente on the other. The old village of San Lorenzo alle Grotte was located in the lowlands closer to Lake Bolsena than the current village. This ancient hamlet was named after the numerous surrounding caves inhabited by the Etruscans. According to local legend, the inhabitants asked for protection from the heavens during the 5th century invasions of the Vandals, and on the feast of Saint Apollinare, a dense fog came down and the invaders spared the town.

San Lorenzo alle Grotte had been always of strategic importance, owing to its position along the via Cassia and a point of contention for local noblemen and The Church. In the year 1113 the area was donated to the Church by Matilda of Canossa, countess of Tuscany, but the same area was sacked by the Holy Roman Emperor Henry VI in 1186. The opposition of Pope Celestine III, mediated by the bishop of Sovana, is recorded in a document dated 28 June 1183. The new town was built in the year 1774, because the lower position of San Lorenzo alle Grotte made it unhealthy for its inhabitants. People were affected by malaria and other epidemics and as a consequence trade ceased. After numerous attempts to decontaminate the area, Cardinal Giovanni Angelo Braschi persuaded Pope Clement XIV to have all the homes moved to a higher and more liveable site. A wide upland in the vicinity of the old village (in a location named Gabelletta) was identified and mandated with a signed document dated June 3, 1772. Pope Clement XIV commissioned the work of reconstruction to architect Francesco Navone, who designed an ideal city according to urban planning canons of his time.

Of particular interest:

The Basilica of Sant'Apollinare Nuovo is a UNESCO World Cultural Heritage site. An early 6th century construction, it was originally dedicated as an Arian church to Christ the Redeemer, then it was re-dedicated as a Roman Catholic Church to Sant'Apollinare Nuovo after the relics of the saint were moved there. The exterior of the church is rather plain and unremarkable apart from a rather attractive cylindrical campanile of Ottonian design, probably erected in the 10th century. The simple marble arcade is from the 16th century when many of the mosaics in the church were destroyed. The Basilica is interesting for its fusion of eastern and western styles. The mosaics are clearly Byzantine in character, while the long nave without transept is more typically Italian in style.

The interior of the basilica is almost bare, which helps to draw attention to the overwhelming mosaics on the upper lateral walls on both sides of the nave. Even though a large number of them were lost to earthquakes, wars, building alterations and botched restorations, the remaining art works are amongst the most impressive in Italy.

Looking from the top down, the mosaics can be divided into three horizontal bands. The upper band, above window level, dates from the reign of Theodoric the Great, and showing the life of Christ (left wall) and the Passion (right wall) in thirteen panels on each side of the nave. Typically, Arian, Christ is still beardless on the left wall. This is less common in the orthodox tradition but not unknown. Other Arian symbols were removed when the basilica became Roman Catholic. The middle band shows biblical figures alternating with windows. As with the upper band, these mosaics date from the time of Theodoric the Great, and are in the Greek Roman style of individualistic facial features, in addition to each figure being shown with different items and symbols. The lower band is more Byzantine in style, with the figures lacking individuality and mostly dating from around half a century later. The Church of Capuchin Fathers is dedicated to a Capuchin friar, Saint Seraphim of Montegranaro. Built in the early 18th century, it was part of a convent of the Capuchin Fathers until 1810, when all religious orders were suppressed by Napoleon I.

Saint Apollinaris

According to tradition, Saint Apollinaire was a native of Antioch, in the Roman Province of Syria, and was made Bishop of Ravenna, Italy, by Saint Peter himself. The miracles he delivered there soon attracted the attention of his Roman rulers. Legends tell that he was cruelly beaten and found half-dead on the seashore, compelled to walk on burning coals, hacked with knives, had scalding water poured over his wounds, was beaten in the mouth with stones because he persisted in preaching, and flung into a dungeon and left to starve, though he was in fact smuggled out and put on board a ship and sent to Greece. When he returned to Ravenna three years later, Vespasian was Emperor, and he issued a decree of banishment against all Christians. Apollinaris was kept concealed for some time, but was ultimately set upon and savagely beaten. Once again, he was rescued and hidden by his Christian followers, but this time the injuries were too severe and he died after seven days.

Lazio

The Italian word Lazio originates from the Latin word *latus*, meaning wide and expressing the idea of a flat land. Today, Lazio is the most populated region in Italy, and the centre of Italian political and religious life, thanks to the presence of the Parliament, but also the Vatican, in Rome. Although originally poor, there has been extensive investment in the region since it joined with the rest of unified Italy in 1870. Now contributing ten percent of the country's GDP, Lazio derives most of its wealth from tourism, agriculture, wine production, manufacturing, textiles, pharmaceuticals, and publishing. Lazio is also home to the Italian film industry. To the east, Lazio is dominated by the Central Apennine mountain ranges, rising to 2,216 metres at Mount Terminillo. To the west, the coast of Lazio is mainly low-lying with long, sandy beaches interrupted by the headlands of Circeo and Gaeta.

Although the history of the region includes stories of wealth and power, especially when it comes to the Eternal City, Rome, Lazio's history is really an intersection of different cultures. Examples of cultural exchange date back to the Etruscans, and are certainly reflected in the regional cooking. The food of Lazio is made up of plain dishes. Sauces used for pasta dishes, vary from the very simple *cacio e pepe*, to much more elaborate recipes that include butter, egg, *pancetta* (an Italian bacon made of salt cured pork belly meat or *guanciale (*an Italian cured meat product prepared from pork jowl or cheeks). The traditional pasta sauce, *Amatriciana*, is made by sautéing onions in pork fat. Rice is also popular, particularly rice balls filled with mozzarella or chicken giblets. However, beef is the meat of choice and *Coda alla Vaccinara*, or braised oxtail, a popular dish. Much of the fish consumed in Lazio comes from the Tiber River and Bolsena Lake. Finally, Lazio is famous for its sheep's milk *pecorinos (cheese)* and sweet ricotta, which is used in many desserts and fillings.

Lazio's vine heritage is ancient, though it was only in the 1870s, when Rome became the capital of Italy, that the wine region flourished once again. Today, Lazio's reputation is mainly based on its white wines, the mainstays being Trebbiano and Malvasia di Candia.

While it is fairly certain Bolsena is the successor to the ancient Roman town of Volsinii, scholarly opinion is sharply divided as to whether *Volsinii* was the same as the ancient Etruscan city of *Velzna* or *Velsuna* (sometimes termed *Volsinii Veteres - Old Volsinii*), the other candidate being Orvieto, twenty kilometres to the north-east. Other historians have pointed out that the town of Bolsena has no Etruscan characteristics. For example, Etruscan cities were built on defensible crags, which the castle is not. The Roman historian Pliny the Elder decided that a bolt from Mars fell and burned it down entirely. As a consequence, he maintained, the population moved to another site, which is thought to be Bolsena.

The town is best known for the lake in front of it. Of volcanic origin, Lake Bolsena was formed by the collapse of a caldera into a deep aquifer. Roman historic records indicate activity of the Vulsini volcano as recently as 104 BC, since when it has been dormant. The two islands in the southern part of the lake were formed by underwater eruptions following the initial collapse.

Bolsena is also known for the Miracle of Bolsena, which occurred in 1263. A Bohemian priest, who was somewhat sceptical about the doctrine of transubstantiation, became convinced of its truth after seeing the miraculous appearance of drops of blood on the host he had just consecrated. The miraculous event was reported to Pope Urban IV, who instituted the feast of Corpus Christi in the following year, and planned the erection of the Cathedral of Orvieto, the town where he resided. The Duomo di Orvieto was eventually built to commemorate the miracle.

One third of the lake was donated to The Church by the noble family Alberici of Orvieto. In recognition of the donation the Alberici family was honoured with a ceremony three times a year, performed by the Bishop of Orvieto.

From April to September, excursion boats offer rides to the islands. Both are privately owned and Martana is not open to the public, but Bisentina is an ex-summer residence of the Popes and has a large church on it. There are also seven small chapels built around the island. One of them contains some beautiful frescoes attributed to Benozzo Gozzoli or his school. The chapels were originally built to make it easier to get a plenary indulgence, by giving pilgrims an alternative to having to visit each of the seven major churches in Rome.

During the Middle Ages, Lake Bolsena was known as Lago di S. Cristina, due to the fact that St. Christina of Bolsena, a 3rd century young martyr, was thrown into the lake tied to a slab of stone, because she refused to abandon her Christian beliefs. However, instead of dragging her down, the stone supported and carried her to shore. A stone with the imprint of the saint's feet is venerated in a 9th century altar inside a cave, which was eventually turned into a shrine. The ancient Romans used to celebrate the safe return from a journey by dedicating similar stones to Rediculus, the god who protected travellers. The centre of the Roman town was located in the northern part of the current Bolsena. Archaeologists have identified the sites of baths, temples, a small theatre and an amphitheatre.

Of particular interest:

The Basilica of Santa Cristina Collegiata is noted for its elegant façade, built in 1492 and financed by Cardinal Giovanni de Medici when he was legate of Patrimonium Petri, the region around Viterbo. Its neat design is probably by Francesco and Benedett Buglioni, two Florentine ceramicists. The reliefs, which decorate the pillars, were inspired by paintings discovered in the Domus Aurea in Rome.

The influence of the Florentine Renaissance shows up in the glazed terracottas on the portals of the Church. St. Christina is portrayed carrying the stone of her martyrdom, while St. Leonard of Noblac was the patron saint of prisoners, which explains his portrayal carrying handcuffs.

Rocca Monaldeschi della Cervara, sits on the top of the hill, overlooking the Medieval quarter of town. The castle was built between the 12th and 14th centuries and has since been completely renovated. Today, it is home to the Museo Territoriale del Lago di Bolsena, each of its three floors dedicated to various aspects of Bolsena's history, ranging from its prehistoric volcanic origins to its Etruscan-Roman period. Your author recommends a walk along the ramparts of the castle, which offer a gorgeous view of the entire lake.

The high ground of Mount Volsini continues to offer beautiful views of the lake, and the route passes through open pastureland and woodland. Encouragement for the footsore and weary comes from signs indicating that there are only 100 kilometres to go before reaching Rome.

Basilica of San Flaviano

Standing to the left of the route and slightly higher up a steep slope, it is easy to either miss the Church of San Flaviano, or dismiss it for its slightly forbidding exterior. San Flaviano, is in fact a peculiar Romanesque temple of the 11th century, consisting of two churches one built on the other, but facing in opposite directions. The façade, built in 1262, has three Gothic portals, surmounted by a 16th century lodge. Inside, there are a number of frescoes from the 13th century, among them an interesting I*ncontro dei Tre Vivi e dei Tre Morti*, and at the centre of the vault a wide opening connecting to the upper church. The lower church hosts the tomb of the German bishop, Johannes Defuk, a renowned enologist who, while on his way to Rome in 1113 AD, sent his valet around the town to find the inns which served good wine, and write the Latin words *est* (there is) on the doors. The valet was so enthusiastic about the local wine that he wrote "est" three times, and with exclamation marks! Coming back from Rome, Defuk drank too much of

the wine and died, leaving a legacy to the town of 24,000 silver coins, on condition that on the anniversary of his death a small casket of wine would be poured on his tomb, where an inscription says: *For the excessive EST! here lies my lord Johannes Defuk.* A local wine label takes its name from the legend.

Finally, if your author's experience is anything to go by, when you enter the church you will be greeted by at least two people who are in charge of the church's maintenance, and possibly a priest. All of them keen to stamp your pilgrim passport.

Montefiascone VII Sce Flaviane

Montefiascone derives its name from the *Falisci*, an ancient population that probably had a citadel here. It was later under the Etruscans who, according to the legends, had a temple there, *Fanum Voltumnae*, where the chiefs of the Dodecapolis (the twelve main Etruscan towns) met for their reunions. The name Montefiascone is mentioned in 853 AD, as a possession of the bishop of Tuscania.

The periods of highest splendour were the 13th and 14th centuries, when the castle was often a residence of Popes, and in the Avignon period it was the residence of Cardinal Albornoz, the Pope's representative in Italy. A slow decline began afterwards, and the situation worsened after the 1657 plague and an earthquake some decades later in 1697.

Of particular interest:

Montefiascone Cathedral or the Basilica of Santa Margherita is one of the most important churches in the area, and has one of the largest domes in Italy, which is visible from most of the towns of the Viterbo area. When Pope Urban V established the Diocese of Montefiascone in 1396, the church that was the most popular and most central was chosen to be the cathedral of the new diocese, after which major reconstruction began. The building from the crypt up to the base of the dome dates from the 15th and 16th centuries and was undertaken by the Veronese architect Michele Sanmicheli, probably with the help of Antonio da Sangallo the Younger. At this time the lower church was created, and the plans for the upper church drawn up, but for economic reasons this phase of building stopped at the level of the roof, and the cathedral remained open to the elements until 1602.

After a fire destroyed the roof and part of the interior of the cathedral, the repair and completion of the construction was entrusted to Carlo Fontana, who produced a dome more in keeping with contemporary taste. The bell towers and west front were designed and added in 1840 by the architect Paul Gazola, using very simple elements of decoration. Besides a marble statue and some relics of Saint Margaret of Antioch, the cathedral contains the relics of Saint Lucia Filippini and the tomb of Cardinal Marco Antonio Barbarigo.

The Lombard penetration from the north favoured the consolidation of a road connected with the via Cassia in Bolsena by passing through the Siena valleys. This was the first stage of the next via Francigena, which allowed northern European pilgrims to reach Rome. The ancient via Cassia is intact for long stretches and is probably the closest today's pilgrim can get to the pilgrims who would have passed through in Sigeric's time. Your author found this stretch probably the most compelling and evocative, particularly because by this time Rome is less than one hundred kilometres away.

Pliny the Elder

Born Gaius Plinius Secundus, AD 23–79, Pliny was a Roman author, naturalist, philosopher, naval and army commander of the early Roman Empire, and friend of emperor Vespasian. At the age of twenty-three, he began a military career serving in Germany and rising to the rank of cavalry commander. He returned to Rome, where he possibly studied law and served in Rome, until near the end of Nero's reign. After this, he became procurator in Spain, during which he lived in semi-retirement, and devoted his time to studying and writing.

Pliny is most notable for the encyclopaedic *Naturalis Historia*, which became an editorial model for encyclopaedias. The Natural History, was divided into 37 *libri*, or books, and completed in 77 CE. In the preface, Pliny justified the title and explained his purpose as being the study of "the nature" of things, that is, life". From here, he continued to explain that no one had attempted to bring together the older, scattered material that belonged to "encyclic culture" (*enkyklios paideia*, the origin of the word encyclopaedia). Disdaining high literary style and political mythology, Pliny adopted a plain style, but one with an unusually rich vocabulary. A novel feature of the work is the care taken in naming his sources, more than one hundred of which are mentioned.

Book II of the Natural History, is devoted to cosmology and astronomy. In Books III through VI, Pliny focuses on the physical and historical geography of the ancient world, including major cities, some of which no longer exist. Books VII through XI treat zoology, beginning with humans (VII), then mammals and reptiles (VIII), fishes and other marine animals (IX), birds (X), and insects (XI).

Pliny's last military assignment was as commander of the fleet in the Bay of Naples. Learning of an unusual cloud formation, later found to have resulted from an eruption of Mount Vesuvius, Pliny went ashore to ascertain the cause and reassure the terrified citizens. Unfortunately, he was overcome by the fumes resulting from the volcanic activity, and died unmarried and survived by his only sister.

In a period in which the popes had difficulties asserting their authority over Rome, Viterbo became their favourite residence, beginning with Pope Eugene III (1145–1146). In 1164, Frederick Barbarossa made Viterbo the seat of his antipope Paschal III and three years later gave it the title of *city* and used its militias against Rome. In 1172, Viterbo started its expansion, destroying the old city of Ferento and conquering other lands. In this age it was a rich and prosperous comune, one of the most important of Central Italy, with a population of almost 60,000.

Today, in spite of sustaining serious bomb damage during World War II, Viterbo's historic centre is one of the best preserved Medieval towns in central Italy. Many of the older buildings (particularly churches) are built on top of ancient ruins, recognizable by their large stones. Viterbo is also often mentioned in the itineraries and chronicles of the journeys of illustrious people, who were not always motivated by veneration - for example, Charles the Great and Charles VIII. Although the old via Cassia did not pass directly through the city, the transit of pilgrims expanded the local economy and established Viterbo's role as a significant commercial centre for the region. In San Pellegrino, Viterbo's oldest and best preserved quarter, Medieval houses with towers, arches and external staircases line narrow streets running between little piazzas decorated with fountains.

Of particular interest:

The Palazzo dei Papi or Papal Palace, hosted the papacy for about two decades in the 13th century, and served as a country residence or refuge in times of trouble in Rome. The columns of the palace were taken from a Roman temple.

The Cathedral of San Lorenzo was originally erected as the episcopal See of the exempt bishopric of Viterbo, and built in Romanesque style by Lombard architects at the site of a Roman temple dedicated to Hercules. It was rebuilt from the 16th century on, but heavily damaged in 1944 by Allied bombs. The Gothic belfry was built in the first half of the 14th century, and shows the influence of Sienese architects. The church houses the sarcophagus of Pope John XXI and a picture of Christ Blessing (1472) by Gerolamo da Cremona.

Palazzo Farnese, a 14th century palace, was the childhood home of Alessandro Farnese, the future Pope Paul III, and his sister, Giulia Farnese.

The Church of San Francesco is a Gothic church built over a pre-existing Lombard fortress, it has a single nave with a Latin cross plan and houses the sepulchre of Pope Adrian V, who died in Viterbo in 1276.

The civic museum houses many archaeological items from pre-historic to Ancient Roman times, plus a *Pinacoteca* (picture gallery) with works by Sebastiano del Piombo, Antoniazzo Romano, Salvator Rosa, Antiveduto Grammatica and others.

The Orto Botanico dell'Università della Tuscia is a botanical garden, created and managed by the university, was established in 1985 and officially inaugurated in 1991.

Santa Maria Rosa

Santa Maria Rosa, patron saint of Viterbo (1235-1252) was born in

Viterbo, Italy. Rosa was remarkable for her holiness and miraculous powers from her earliest years. When only three-years-old, she is said to have raised her maternal aunt from death. At the age of seven, she had already lived the life of a recluse, devoting herself to penances. Her health was poor, but she was reputed to have been cured by the Blessed Virgin Mary, who ordered her to enroll herself in the Third Order of Francis of Assisi and to preach penance to Viterbo, at that time (1247) held by Frederick II, Holy Roman Emperor, and prey to political strife and heresy.

Her mission seems to have extended for about two years and such was her success that the prefect of the city decided to banish her. Accordingly, Rose and her parents were expelled from Viterbo in January 1250, and took refuge in Soriano nel Cimino. On 5th December 1250, Rose foretold the speedy death of the emperor, a prophecy realised on 13th December. Soon afterwards she went to Vitorchiano, whose inhabitants, according to surviving reports, were affected by a supposed sorceress. Rose secured the conversion of all, even of the sorceress, by standing unscathed for three hours in the flames of a burning pyre.

With the restoration of the papal power in Viterbo (1251) Rose returned. She wanted to enter the monastery of St. Mary of the Roses, but was refused because of her poverty. She accepted her rejection, but foretold that she would be admitted to the monastery after her death. The remainder of her life was spent in a cell in her father's house, where she died. Her feast is celebrated on 4th September, when her body (believed by the faithful to be still whole and uncorrupted, despite the passage of time), is carried in procession through Viterbo.

Beyond Viterbo the old route crossed the Arcione over a Roman bridge, today referred to as San Nicolao, passing very near two important castles: Castel d'Asso and Castel di Salce, both of which were involved in the wars between Viterbo and Rome. A hospital was founded at Risiere, along the via Cassia, in the middle of the 12th century, and the surrounding plain was often the site of military encampments. After passing close-by to Petrignano, the old route went through Santa Maria di Forcassi built on the corresponding site of Forum Cassii (listed as Furcassi by Sigeric).

The Bagnaccio

Heated by the earth's core and bubbling out of the ground, this natural volcanic spring, set in open fields, has been channelled into a series of shallow bathing pools – each with a different temperature. The site is best known as the *Bagnaccio*, which roughly translates as 'nasty old bath'. The Romans used to bathe here and the site has changed remarkably little in two thousand years. The Bagnaccio isn't the only outdoor hot spring for bathing near Viterbo, but its raw simplicity might make it the most charming.

Today's current via Francigena route has taken you along Roman roads, with the paving barely altered since it was used by Roman troops, merchants and pilgrims. Now you will follow the via Cava di Sant'Antonio, a magnificent road dug deep into the tufa stone by the Etruscans. The name comes from the chapel you will pass. The walls of the via Cave are over fifteen metres high and bear symbols and inscriptions.

Vetralla V Furcari

Local legend says that Vetralla dates back to the biblical figure of Noah, who ran the Ark aground on the heights of Valle Cajana, and availed himself of the excellent wines found there. No one can be sure, but we do know that Etruria was populated by the Etruscans who left their mark in various tomb cities scattered throughout the entire region. Vetralla sits on the slope of Mount Fogliano, at the crossroads of three important Roman roads - via Cassia, via Clodio, and via Aurelia. A relatively short distance from Rome, it became an important Roman outpost. Over the centuries, Vetralla was passed around as a trophy among the nobility of various epochs and was finally donated by Pope Julius II to England's ambassador of King Henry VIII, remaining under British protection for hundreds of years. Today's historic centre is a well-preserved example of Medieval civic construction, retaining its sinewy alleyways and stone houses clustered together, interspersed with many tiny piazzas.

Right outside Vetralla there are some fascinating necropoli, the Norchia, carved into the cliffs, along with hand-formed stone passageways.

Of particular interest:

The Cathedral of Sant'Andrea is known for the Madonna of the Rosary, attributed to Ludovico Mazzanti and the Crucifixion of St. Andrew by Domenico Muratori. There is also an outstanding 12th century panel of the Madonna Intercessor (on the reverse, the Head of the Saviour). A small crystal shrine houses several reliquaries, including one in silver gilt by Giovanni Anastasio di Vitale, and a small silvered urn with the relics of St. Hippolytus.

The Romanesque, 11th century Church of San Francesco has an elegant Cosmati portal and, most notably, 16th and 17th century frescoes on the walls of the central nave and in the presbytery, with stories on the life of St. Francis by Francesco Villamena 1566-1624.

The City and Territories museum has exhibits dedicated to the history and traditional handicrafts of Tuscia.

Capranica

Legend has it that in the 8th century AD, goatherds from the village of Vicus Matrini fled a Lombard invasion and settled on the tuff hill, which they chose for safety and healthy air. This settlement became known as Capranica, *capra* meaning goat.

Capranica lies in the historic area of Tuscia, which is the ancient name for Southern Etruria, the land of the Etruscans and the heartland of the greatest civilisation in pre-Roman and early Roman Italy (9th-3rd century BC). The Etruscans left an abundance of archaeological remains, mostly necropoles, all around Capranica.

Much later, in the year 800, Charlemagne, king of the Franks and Italy, crossed Capranica on his way to Rome to be crowned Emperor of the Romans. He may have followed the via Francigena.

The next mention of Capranica, was by Francesco Petrarca (in English

known as Petrarch), a scholar, poet and one of the earliest humanists, who spent a month in Capranica as a guest of the noble House of Anguillara, and wrote of bold farmers there who, as they worked their fields, always had a sword and a spear lying in the ruts ready to defend themselves and their homes.

Capranica is situated on a hill overlooking the Sutri valley, and consists of three distinct parts. Castrovecchio is the Medieval and oldest part of Capranica, its narrow, winding streets, small piazzas and noble palazzi guarded by precipitous drops and formidable defence walls within the two main gates: Porta San Pietro on the east, and Porta del Ponte on the west, where it blends with the ancient Anguillara castle. To the west of this gate the Renaissance (1380–1600) section of Capranica is closed off from the newest section of the town, which lies outside the town walls. Your route, along the via Francigena runs alongside them.

In 1800 to 1815, Napoleon's regime brought improved laws and

administration to Capranica, but also military conscription, forced participation in distant and bloody wars, and the deportation of those who wanted to remain loyal to the old regime. Meanwhile, Giuseppe Mazzini, politician, journalist and activist for the unification of Italy, and an advocate of a United States of Europe, a century before the European Union began to take shape, passed through Capranica on his way to Rome and expressed much admiration for the volcanic landscape and the Etruscan rock tombs alongside the road.

Of particular interest:

The Portal of St Sebastian's hospital, which belonged to the 13th century Church of San Giovanni.

The Church of San Francesco with Michelangelo-style frescoes and a tomb effigy by Pietro da Gualdo of Francesco and Nicola Anguillara.

Capranica's cathedral, the Church of San Giovanni, was reconstructed in its current form in 1800, but retains its 16th century dome and the original 13th century bell tower.

The Church of San Rocco (15th century), now houses the Museum of the Confraternity.

The Church of Santa Maria, designed by the architect Renzo Vespignani in 1867, houses several important paintings: the Benedictory Saviour (12–13th century), a triptych depicting St Terentian, St Roch, St Sebastian and the statue of Madonna delle Grazie (1808).

Anguillara Torrione Castle, with its Clock Bridge and portal, Porta del Ponte dell'Orologio.

Madonna del Piano was built in 1559–87, and with its splendid façade is attributed to Giacomo Barozzi da Vignola, the author of The Five Orders of Architecture.

Porta di Sant'Antonio (St Anthony's Gate), erected in the 17th century by Cardinal Antonio Barberini.

Palazzo Montenero-Sansoni, erected in the second half of the 18th century by a French doctor of medicine, Charles Thierry, as a sanatorium for treatment with mineral waters. Thierry had analysed the properties of mineral water in Capranica, and in 1766 published his work as Les Eaux Minerales de Capranica.

Petrach

Petrarch was a poet and scholar whose humanist philosophy set the stage for the Renaissance. Petrarch was born Francesco Petrarca on July 20, 1304, in Arezzo, Tuscany. He was a devoted classical scholar, considered the Father of Humanism, a philosophy that set the stage for the Renaissance. His writing was also used to shape the modern Italian language.

Petrarch became a cleric, making him eligible for ecclesiastical postings, which supported him as he pursued his interest in ancient literature. Travelling as a diplomatic envoy for the Church, he was also able to search for forgotten classical texts. As he learned more about the classical period, he began to venerate that era and rail against the limitations of his own time.

Petrarch was a passionate writer. His first pieces were poems composed after the death of his mother, but he would go on to write sonnets, letters, histories and more. Petrarch's writing was greatly admired during his lifetime, and he was crowned Rome's poet laureate in 1341.

Petrarch's most well-known vernacular compositions were lyrical poems about Laura, a woman he had fallen in, unrequited, love with after seeing her in an Avignon church. He wrote about Laura, whose true identity has never actually been verified for most of his life, even after she died during the Black Death of 1348. Petrarch died just before his 70th birthday.

Sutri IlIl Suteria

After Capranica the road comes to Sutri, recorded as *Suteria* by Sigeric, but also listed as a staging post by Nicola de Munkatveà, Philip Augustus, Abnnales Stadenses, Charles the Great, Hugh of Provence and Otto II. The town's prosperity is closely linked to its position on the via Cassia in Roman times and on the via Francigena in the Middle Ages. Titus Livius, known as Livy in English, was a Roman historian who wrote a monumental history of Rome and the Roman people, describing Sutri as being one of the keys of Etruria, Nepi being the other. The settlement came into the hands of Rome after the fall of Veii, and a Latin colony was founded in the 12th century, Sutri being ruled as a municipality and often allied with Rome against Viterbo. In 1236 the destruction of the city bridge prompted Pope Gregory IX to allow the town to impose tolls for the restoration of the bridge and the maintenance of the roads. But from the 15th century, the increased use of the alternative route to Ronciglione, brought about the decline of Sutri and Vetralla.

Picturesquely situated on a narrow tuff hill and surrounded by ravines, Sutri is best known for its Roman amphitheatre and Etruscan necropolis. These consist of dozens of rock-cut tombs and a *Mithraeum* (a place of worship for the followers of the religion of Mithraism), incorporated in the crypt of its church of the Madonna del Parto.

The amphitheatre is completely carved out of local tufa stone. Although it is fairly small, it faces the town as it did in ancient times and offers an enchanting, almost mystical atmosphere. Opinions vary as to exactly when it was built, ranging from as early as the Etruscan archaic period to the first decades of the Christian era.

Built on a north-south axis, it has two entrances at its farthest extremities and its shape is slightly oval. A tunnel, with five entrances still visible on each side, circles the area at its outer circumference, thus separating it from the spectators' section, the *cavea*, which was divided into three orders of tiers. A rectangular niche cut into the lowest section on the northwest side had its own private entrance and is believed to be the VIP seat, or what we might call the royal box.

Sutri's municipal cemetery, alongside the amphitheatre, dates from the ancient Roman period and features a variety of tombs including the single chamber, double chamber, arched entrance and rectangular niche varieties. Not all are visible, because many were badly damaged when used by local farmers as storage for farm equipment, or even as pig sties. A particularly unusual feature of this necropolis is the way in which it was used for both burial and cremation ceremonies over successive periods of time. After first belonging to wealthy Etruscans, it was then used by the Romans, later converted into a temple by the Mithraic cult and finally adopted by the Christians. The first of its two rooms is small and square and was probably a vestibule. The second room is long and rectangular, with benches. Christians frequently built churches over Mithraic shrines (e.g Rome's Santa Prisca and San Clemente) or pagan temples. Thus, in the 6th or 7th century AD, Sutri's Mithraic shrine became a church dedicated to the Madonna del Parto. The earliest frescoes in the church date from this period and are to be found on the two pilasters closest to the altar.

The upper part of Sutri is on higher ground and, notwithstanding the fact that it is now occupied by the Cathedral and by Palazzo Vescovile, it still conveys the image of a fortress. The main Medieval buildings of Sutri retain something of the Etruscan and Roman times and this applies to the whole town.

Of particular interest:

Sutri has some interesting signs of the Baroque period. For example, a 17th century clock in the centre of the town, which is still set to indicate the Italian hour, showing six rather than twelve hours and just one pointer (in this clock a ray of the sun). The pointer reached six at sunset in every period of the year, because the clock was reset every two weeks to take care of the changes in the duration of daylight, meaning that the Italian hour was indicating what was left of the day before sunset.

Sutri, but even more Monterosi, was serviced by the alternative route of the via Francigena, which came into use in the late Middle Ages. Beyond Viterbo, passing the Cistercian abbey of San Martino al Cimino, it skirted the eastern shores of Lake Vico, and passed through Ronciglione, recorded for the first time as late as 1243 when it belonged to the counts Anguillara. Another variant of the via Francigena passed through Nepi, but the main route, after skirting round lake Monterosi, passed through the castle of the same name (Castrum Montis Rosi), which is occasionally recorded as a staging post and, because it was built outside the walls on land belonging to the monastery of San Paolo, became the contentious property of various Roman families. Its surroundings were the setting for the misdeeds of a Sienese adventurer, Giovanni Malavolta. One account claims that after witnessing the assault of some Rome-bound pilgrims, Malavolta killed a number of their attackers and then robbed them all.

Mithraism

Mithraism was a mystery cult in the Roman world, where followers worshipped the Indo-Iranian deity, Mithras, as the god of friendship, contract and order. The cult first appeared in the late 1st century CE and spread from the Italian Peninsula and border regions across the whole of the Roman empire. The cult, like many others, was a secret one. Votaries worshipped Mithras in temples often built into caves and hidden away from the public. However, the cult was tolerated by the authorities, especially by the Roman emperors, because it was in favour of imperial power. Over two hundred Mithras temples have been found, stretching from Syria to Britain, but finds are concentrated mostly in Italy, on the banks of rivers Rhine and Danube. After the establishment of Christianity, the Mithras Mysteries diminished in importance and its temples either walled up or destroyed. However, some temples remained in use until the early 5th century CE.

Other important elements of the cult were self-denial and a moral questioning of the self. For example, a crown was placed on the initiate's head, which he had to reject, saying "Mithras is my (true) crown". The earliest documented followers of Mithras were soldiers and officers of the Roman army, but with the rising popularity of the cult, the majority of votaries were successful, freed slaves of the cities. Women, however, were excluded.

The most important element of the myth behind the Mithraic Mysteries was Mithras' killing of a bull, known as *tauroctony*. It was believed that new life came from the death of the bull - an animal often seen as a symbol of strength and fertility. Rebirth was an essential component of the Mithraic Mysteries. The sacrifice of the bull was believed to establish a new cosmic order and was also associated with the moon, which in turn represented fertility.

The sacrifice of the bull was depicted in a stone relief that always held a central position in the temples. In the relief, Mithras is often shown as he wrangles the bull to the ground. Being a Persian god, Mithras wears the Phrygian cap and pants, which were not worn by Romans. Around six-hundred-and-fifty of these stone reliefs have been found, and they are all strikingly similar.

Monterosi

The region is characterized by a number of lakes of volcanic origin. The smallest ones have been drained at different stages, with the exception of the circular pond near the little town of Monterosi. In the past Monterosi was just a handful of houses along the via Cassia, but in spite of this it is home to a large palace built in 1690 by Giovanni Battista Contini for the Altieri family.

Monte Gelato Falls

Your route takes you through beautiful parkland and past one of the most picturesque points in the Treja valley. The site has been inhabited since prehistoric times, but there are also the remains of a Roman villa from the 1st century BC. Look out for the watermill from 1830, which was active until the 1960s and is now open as a venue for a permanent exhibition on the territory.

Campagnano di Roma

The first documentation of Borgo di Campagnano dates from 1076, when it was defined as a *castellum*, having been carved out of the great estate assembled on the Roman pattern by Pope Adrian I (ca. 780) - his *Domuscula Caprarorum*. It was cited again in 1130, among the properties of the monastery of San Paolo. Campagnano remained relatively autonomous until 1410 when it entered into the possession of the Orsini family. In 1662, the village passed to the Chigi, who between 1600 and 1700, enlarged the Medieval centre. In 1818, Campagnano became a municipality and participated actively in the birth of the Kingdom of Italy to which it was annexed in 1870. The current town is composed of three distinct sectors: the modern sector, the Renaissance-Baroque sector and the Medieval sector, which is located at the extremities of the plateau and is rich in towers, palaces and churches.

If you are there in April May, you could enjoy the *Palio delle Contrade,* a costumed parade, which is followed by a race of dignitaries on donkeys representing the town's districts and battling it out for the prized *Palio* (a painted drapery). Alternatively, there is the Festa del Baccanale in May, a 55-year tradition of culinary, wine, and artisan highlights.

Of particular interest:

The Church of San Giovanni Battisti built in 1515 and featuring some fine frescoes.

The archaeological museum shows off artefacts found in the area, which was an Etruscan zone before being taken over by the Romans.

Fontana dei Delfini built in Baroque style with travertine dolphins next to a large peperino bell.

PRO LOCO
FORMELLO
2011-2017
VF
ROMA
KM 27.3

Formello

This is the last town you will pass through before Rome. Located on a small hill, it was originally under the control of the Etruscan city of Veii. The Etruscans built a dense network of tunnels to drain the water of the Tiber. The Romans built many villas and farms in this rural area, until everything was abandoned with the decline of the empire.

From the 8th century, The Church began to repopulate the area under Pope Adrian I, and some new *domusculta* or agricultural colonies, were formed in the Roman style, the so-called *Domusculta Capracorum*. With the arrival of the Barbarian invasions, the population left the valley and settled on the heights, and in this period the actual center of Formello was formed under the protection of the Monastery of St. Paul Outside the Walls. Pope Nicholas III assigned Formello to the Orsini family, and in 1661 the fiefdom of Formello was finally sold to the Chigi family.

Of particular interest:

The 10th century Church of San Lorenzo, with its beautiful 18th century sundial.

La Storta Il Johannis VIIII

La Storta has gained its notability thanks to Ignatius of Loyola, who

was travelling the Via Cassia towards Rome in 1537, accompanied by Peter Faber and Diego Laynez. The group paused at a small church in La Storta to pray, and it was there that Ignatius is reported to have received a vision of God the Father and Christ holding the cross. Ignatius later said that Christ spoke the words *Ego tibi Romae propitius ero* ("I will be favourable to you in Rome"). The meaning of the sentence was not immediately clear to Ignatius, who thought it could mean that the three might be martyred in Rome, but thankfully Pope Paul III gave them a very friendly reception.

The location of the apparition is memorialized today with a small chapel dedicated to Saint Ignatius in the Piazza della Visione. The site of the vision was a place of pilgrimage from the early days of the Society of Jesus, but the current form of the chapel was restored and decorated by the Superior General Thyrsus González de Santalla in 1700. The Feast of the Vision of Saint Ignatius is celebrated on the second Sunday of November, and is marked by processions, bands, and a re-enactment of the vision.

Of particular interest:

The Cattedrale dei Sacri Cuori di Gesù e Maria was not completed until Cardinal Tisserant took a personal interest and raised funds from many sources, including the United States. The new cathedral was dedicated on March 25, 1950, and visited by Pope Pius XII on October 27 of the same year.

Montemario Park

The final stage in your journey takes you through the Monte Mario Park, set on the highest hill in a range of hills called Monti della Farnesina - a real mosaic of biological diversity which is rare in cities as vast as Rome.

The hill was known as *Mons Vaticanus* or *Clivus Cinnae* in Roman times, but the current name, according to some theories, comes from Mario Mellini, a cardinal who around the middle of 15th century owned a villa and several hamlets in the area. In the Middle Ages, however, it was known as *Monte Malo* (Bad Mountain), due to the murder of the patrician, Giovanni Crescenzio (998). The eastern part is a nature reserve, which includes the Santa Maria Rosario church and convent. Also visible, and now occupying the site of the 15th century Villa Mellini, is the Rome Observatory and the Museo Astronomico Copernicano. This location (12°27'8.4"E) was used as the prime meridian (rather than Greenwich) for maps of Italy until the 1960s. Although the highest hill in the modern city of Rome, Monte Mario is not one of the proverbial Seven Hills of Rome, because it is outside the boundaries of the ancient city.

Rome Unvisited

I.

The corn has turned from grey to red,
Since first my spirit wandered forth
From the drear cities of the north,
And to Italia's mountains fled.
And here I set my face towards home,
For all my pilgrimage is done,
Although, methinks, yon blood-red sun
Marshals the way to Holy Rome.
O Blessed Lady, who dost hold
Upon the seven hills thy reign!
O Mother without blot or stain,
Crowned with bright crowns of triple gold!
O Roma, Roma, at thy feet
I lay this barren gift of song!
For, ah! the way is steep and long
That leads unto thy sacred street.

II.

And yet what joy it were for me
To turn my feet unto the south,
And journeying towards the Tiber mouth
To kneel again at Fiesole!
And wandering through the tangled pines
That break the gold of Arno's stream,
To see the purple mist and gleam
Of morning on the Apennines.
By many a vineyard-hidden home,
Orchard and olive-garden grey,
Till from the drear Campagna's way
The seven hills bear up the dome!

III.
A pilgrim from the northern seas-
What joy for me to seek alone
The wondrous Temple and the throne
Of Him who holds the awful keys!
When, bright with purple and with gold,
Come priest and holy Cardinal,
And borne above the heads of all
The gentle Shepherd of the Fold.
O joy to see before I die
The only God-anointed King,
And hear the silver trumpets ring
A triumph as He passes by!
Or at the altar of the shrine
Holds high the mystic sacrifice,
And shows a God to human eyes
Beneath the veil of bread and wine.

IV.
For lo, what changes time can bring!
The cycles of revolving years
May free my heart from all its fears,—
And teach my lips a song to sing.
Before yon field of trembling gold
Is garnered into dusty sheaves,
Or ere the autumn's scarlet leaves
Flutter as birds adown the wold,
I may have run the glorious race,
And caught the torch while yet aflame,
And called upon the holy name
Of Him who now doth hide His face.

Oscar Wilde

Rome I Urbs Rom

According to Roman tradition, the city was founded by the twins Romulus and Remus on 21 April 753 BC. Archaeological evidence supports the view that Rome grew from pastoral settlements on the Palatine Hill, built in the area of the future Roman Forum. While some archaeologists argue that Rome was established in the middle of the 8th century BC, the date is subject to controversy. Debate aside, the original settlement clearly developed into the capital of the Roman Kingdom, then the Roman Republic, and finally the Roman Empire. This success depended on military conquest and commercial predominance, as well as selective assimilation of neighbouring civilisations, most notably the Etruscans and Greeks.

From its foundation, Rome remained undefeated in war until 386 BC, when it was briefly occupied by the Gauls. According to legend, the Gauls offered to deliver Rome back to its people for a thousand pounds of gold, but the Romans refused, preferring to take their city back by force of arms rather than ever admitting defeat, after which the Romans did indeed recover their city.

Roman dominance expanded over most of Europe and the shores of the Mediterranean Sea, while its population surpassed one million inhabitants. For almost a thousand years, Rome was the most politically important, richest and largest city in the Western world. After the Empire started to decline and split, it lost its capital status first to Milan, and then to Ravenna, and was finally surpassed in prestige by the Eastern capital of Constantinople.

The Fall of the Empire and the Middle Ages

With the reign of Constantine I, the Bishop of Rome gained political as well as religious importance, eventually becoming known as the Pope and establishing Rome as the centre of the Catholic Church. After the Sack of Rome in 410 AD, by Alaric I, and the fall of the Western Roman Empire in 476 AD, Rome alternated between Byzantine and Germanic control. Its population declined to a mere 20,000 during the Early Middle Ages, reducing the sprawling city to groups of inhabited buildings, interspersed with large areas of ruins and vegetation. Rome remained nominally part of the Byzantine Empire until 751 AD, when the Lombards finally abolished the Exarchate of Ravenna. In 756, Pepin the Short gave the Pope temporal jurisdiction over Rome and its surrounding areas, thus creating the Papal States. In 846, Muslim Arabs invaded Rome and looted St. Peter's Basilica.

Rome remained the capital of the Papal States until its annexation by the Kingdom of Italy in 1870. The city became a major pilgrimage site during the Middle Ages, and the focus of struggles between the Papacy and the Holy Roman Empire starting with Charlemagne, who was crowned its first emperor in Rome by Pope Leo III. Apart from brief periods as an independent city during the Middle Ages, Rome kept its status as Papal capital and 'holy city' for centuries, even when the Papacy briefly relocated to Avignon (1309–1377).

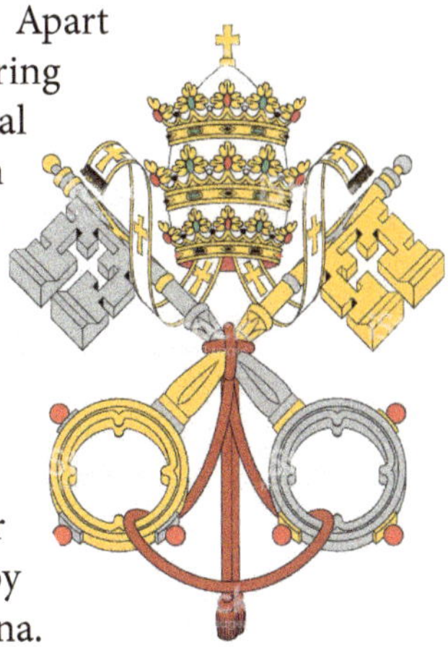

The Rome of the Middle Ages did not remotely resemble the Urbs of the imperial age, nor had it yet acquired the appearance bestowed on it subsequently by the Renaissance and Baroque popes. It had significantly fewer inhabitants than many other cities crossed by the via Francigena, for example Lucca and Siena. In fact, the Medieval town of Rome occupied only a part of the area contained within the Aurelian walls, being concentrated mainly between the Quirinale, the Palatino and the Tiber, with an additional area on the right bank of the river. The huge, early Christian basilicas rose up amidst poor housing, fields and imposing, but disorderly ruins. The splendid monuments of imperial Rome, if not used as churches or fortifications by the major Roman families, simply became a source of building materials and were stripped of their marble, wrought iron and bronze. Nevertheless, to the Medieval man Rome still appeared different. Even the common pilgrim who undertook the long journey to Rome to visit the shrines, could not ignore the glorious ruins of the imperial time exalted by the *Mirabilia urbis Romae*.

Pilgrimages to the Holy Land, which had experienced a considerable boom during the time of Constantine, fell off drastically in the early Middle Ages, especially after the advent of Islam. Consequently, the difficulty of reaching the East favoured Rome. As well as its ancient, though fallen imperial prestige, Rome could boast the primate of the apostolic succession and an indisputable spiritual superiority, corroborated by the remains of numerous martyrs preserved in the catacombs. The Medieval traveller, on his arrival in Rome, entered Borgo Leonino through the city gate of San Pellegrino and found before him the Constantine Basilica of San Pietro, built on the site of the Circus of Nero and replaced in the 16th century with Michelangelo's magnificent church.

One can speculate about the places a Medieval pilgrim would have visited, besides paying homage at the tomb of St. Peter, he would have gone to various other churches – his or her choice being influenced by nationality. Sigeric stopped in Rome for just two days, but nevertheless visited twenty-two churches, besides St. Peter's, starting with Santa Maria della schola Anglorum, which was set up to receive pilgrims from his country. Next, he went to the present day Santo Spirito in Sassia, built between the 7th and 8th centuries for Saxon pilgrims.

The *scholae* were in fact hospices set up near to the Vatican basilica by groups of pilgrims from different countries. These became increasingly numerous as the 'business' of pilgrimages to Rome prospered. On his first day in Rome, after stopping off at his *schola*, Sigeric visited fourteen churches, including San Paolo, San Lorenzo fuori le Mura, San Sebastiano, Santa Sabina and Santa Maria in Trastevere. The next day he began by paying homage in the church of Santa Maria Rotonda and San Giovanni in Laterano, then went on to four other churches, including Santa Croce in Gerusalemme, Santa Maria Maggiore and San Lorenzo in Panisperna, which marked the end of his tour and the beginning of his return journey to Canterbury.

Renaissance Rome

The latter half of the 15th century saw the seat of the Italian Renaissance move to Rome from Florence. The Papacy wanted to equal and surpass the grandeur of other Italian cities and to this end created ever more extravagant churches, bridges and public spaces, including a new Saint Peter's Basilica, the Sistine Chapel, Ponte Sisto (the first bridge to be built across the Tiber since antiquity) and Piazza Navona.

The Popes were also patrons of the arts engaging such artists as Michelangelo, Perugino, Raphael, Ghirlandaio, Luca Signorelli, Botticelli and Cosimo Rosselli. However, the period was also infamous for papal corruption, with many Popes fathering children and engaging in nepotism and simony. The corruption of the Popes and the extravagance of their building projects led, in part, to the Reformation and, in turn, the Counter-Reformation.

The Vatican

Vatican City, the world capital of Catholicism, is the world's smallest state, and occupies one hundred and six acres within high walls watched over by the Vatican guard. Here, where St. Peter was martyred (c.AD 64) and buried, is the residence of the popes who succeeded him.

The Vatican, a sovereign state since 1929, is ruled by the Pope, Europe's only absolute monarch. About five hundred people live in this tiny country,which also has its own post office, banks, currency, radio station, shops, daily newspaper and judicial system. The papal palaces, next to the great Basilica of St Peter's, are home to the Sistine Chapel and the eclectic collections housed in the Vatican Museums.

St Peter's Basilica

Catholicism's most sacred shrine, draws pilgrims and tourists from all over the world. A shrine housing hundreds of precious works of art, some salvaged from the original 4th century basilica built by Constantine, others commissioned from Renaissance and Baroque artists. The dominant tone is set by Bernini, who created the *baldacchino* (a canopy over an altar or throne) twisting up below Michelangelo's huge dome. He also created the cathedra in the apse, with four saints supporting a throne that contains fragments once thought to be relics of the chair from which St. Peter delivered his first sermon.

Vatican Museums

Home to the Sistine Chapel and Raphael Rooms, as well as one of the world's most important art collections, the Vatican Museums are housed in palaces originally intended for Renaissance popes. Most of the latter additions were made in the 18th century, when priceless works of art accumulated by earlier popes were first put on show. The Vatican's greatest treasures are its Greek and Roman antiquities, together with artefacts excavated from Egyptian and Etruscan tombs during the 19th century. Some of Italy's greatest artists, Raphael, Michelangelo and Leonardo de Vinci are represented in the Pinacoteca and parts of the former palaces, where they were previously used by popes to decorate their apartments and galleries.

Sistine Chapel

Michelangelo frescoed the ceiling for Pope Julius II between 1508 and 1512, working from specially designed scaffolding. The main panels, which chart the Creation of the World and Fall of Man, are surrounded by subjects from the Old and New Testaments - except for the Classical Sibyls who are said to have foreseen the birth of Christ.

The recent restorers of the Sistine Chapel used computers, photography and spectrum technology to analyse the fresco before cleaning began.

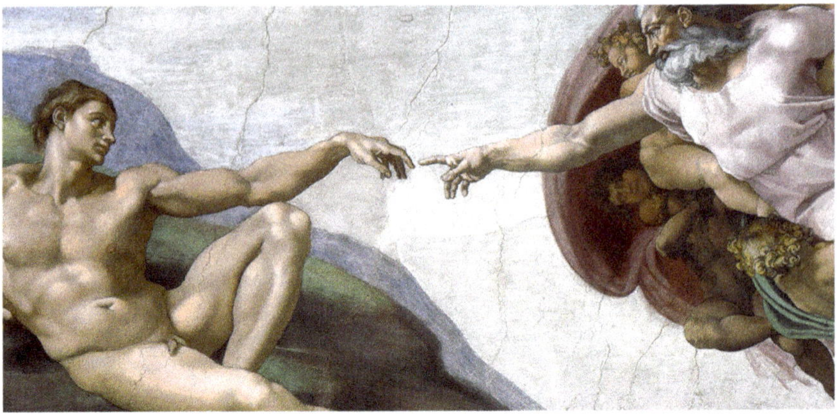

They separated Michelangelo's work from that of the later restorers and discovered that they had attempted to clean the ceiling with materials ranging from bread to retsina wine. The new restoration revealed the familiarly dusky, eggshell-cracked figures to have creamy skins, lustrous hair and brightly-coloured robes. Experts agreed that the new colours probably matched those painted by Michelangelo.

The walls of the Sistine Chapel, the main chapel in the Vatican Palace, were frescoed by some of the finest artists of the 15th and 16th centuries. The twelve paintings on the side walls, by artists including Perugino, Ghirlandalo, Botticelli and Signorelli, show parallel episodes from the life of Moses and of Christ. Decoration was completed between 1534 and 1541 by Michelangelo, who added the great altar wall fresco, The Last Judgement.

Pilgrim Churches of Rome - the Major basilicas

There are traditionally seven designated Pilgrim Churches. The two most important of these are Saint Paul Outside the Walls and of course, Saint Peter's Basilica in the Vatican. But besides visiting the resting places of the pillars of Christianity, pilgrims to Rome also make stops at the other major and minor basilicas.

San Paolo fuori le Mura

Ravaged by fire, floods and earthquakes, the basilica dedicated to Saint Paul still retains its ancient layout. Built on the site of a former graveyard outside the walls of Rome where the martyred Saint Paul was buried, it is much like the tomb of Saint Peter. Saint Paul's grave was also a pilgrimage location marked by centuries of veneration before the church was built. Today, the Benedictine monks of San Paolo fuori le Mura offer services and confessions for pilgrims wishing to venerate Saint Paul and their abbey. The Basilica has a wonderful cloister for contemplation. After a long and turbulent history in which most of the ancient church has been rebuilt, the actual location of Saint Paul was lost somewhere underneath the main altar. At the request of recent pilgrims, excavations by Vatican archaeologists have been carried out in order to make the relics of Saint Paul more accessible to the faithful.

San Giovanni in Laterano

This is the site of the first church allowed by Constantine and is still considered the Mother Church of Roman Catholicism. San Giovanni in Laterano is the Cathedral of Rome and therefore the Church of Rome's Bishop, the Pope. The church has never lost its importance to pilgrims, even though St Peter's has become more important in recent times. Many of the Catholic Church's most important events took place here, and the Lateran Palace was the official Papal residence for centuries. San Giovanni in Laterano and the surrounding area is home to very important relics, including the heads of Saints Peter and Paul housed in the elaborate gothic baldachin of the high altar. The high altar is also said to contain a portion of a table used in masses held by Saint Peter himself. Across the street are the remains of the original Papal palace, which houses both the *Scala Santa*, or Holy Stairs, and the *Sancta Sanctorum*, a series of chapels known for having many holy relics including the Salvatore Acheiropoieton, an icon of Christ supposedly painted by Saint Luke the Evangelist.

Santa Maria Maggiore

The Basilica of Santa Maria Maggiore is the oldest church in Western Europe, dedicated to the Virgin Mary. The church was built on the 5th century site of a miraculous snowfall in the height of Roman summer. Unlike the other ancient basilicas of Rome, Santa Maria Maggiore has not been completely rebuilt and a large amount of the ancient church survives, including original mosaics. The church is the final resting place of Saint Jerome, translator of the Vulgate and houses relics belonging to the Apostle Matthias. Under the high altar lies the Bethlehem Crypt and the relic of the Holy Crib, pieces of wood from the manger of Jesus. Santa Maria Maggiore also houses the Marian icon known as the *Salus Populi Romani*, another holy image that may have been originally painted by Saint Luke. The image, located in the Borghese Chapel has been the object of veneration for pilgrims, popes, saints and especially the citizens of Rome.

Pilgrim Churches of Rome - the Minor Basilicas

San Lorenzo fuori le Mura was built in the year 258, on the site where Lawrence, a Deacon of Rome, was burned to death. The present structure is actually two churches that were combined in the Middle Ages, leaving the basilica with a slightly uneven floor plan. During World War II San Lorenzo was heavily damaged, but has since been faithfully restored. The church is the final resting place of at least three saints: Saint Lawrence, Pope Saint Hilarius and Christian proto-martyr Saint Stephen, all of whom are buried below the high altar. San Lorenzo fuori le Mura also holds a blood-stained stone, where the body of Saint Lawrence was placed before burial.

San Sebastian fuori le Mura

This Basilica is one of the most historically important of the Christian pilgrim sites in Rome. The catacombs under the church were once the temporary resting places of many early Christian martyrs, including Saints Peter and Paul during the Roman persecutions. It was during this time that the saints were interred here and the site became popular with pilgrims. Saint Sebastian was a Roman soldier condemned to death by arrows. Pillaged by the Saracens in the 9th century, nothing remains of the ancient structure, except the catacombs below. Saint Sebastian's body is buried under the altar, while the Chapel of the Relics houses other holy objects, including one of the arrows said to have pierced Saint Sebastian during his martyrdom.

Santa Croce in Gerusalemme

Saint Helena, the mother of Emperor Constantine, built this basilica in the imperial Sessorian palace to house the relics she brought back from the Holy Land. These relics include nails from the Crucifixion, two thorns from the Crown of Thorns, small fragments of the True Cross and the Titulus Crucis, or headboard of the Crucifixion. They were once housed in Saint Helena's personal chapel, but since the church has undergone several redesigns over the centuries, the Relics of the Passion are now housed in the Sanctuary of the Cross. Besides these important relics Santa Croce also houses a finger of the Apostle Thomas.

www.ingramcontent.com/pod-product-compliance
Ingram Content Group UK Ltd.
Pitfield, Milton Keynes, MK11 3LW, UK
UKHW062309290726
14090UKWH00018B/965

9 782917 183380